CHICAGO'S FIRST
CRIME KING

MICHAEL CASSIUS McDONALD

KELLY PUCCI

THE
History
PRESS

D1452746

Published by The History Press
Charleston, SC
www.historypress.com

Cover images courtesy of the Chicago History Museum.

First published 2019

Manufactured in the United States

ISBN 9781467140553

Library of Congress Control Number: 2018966326

To Joe Pucci, for suggesting that I write a book about Michael Cassius McDonald.

CONTENTS

ACKNOWLEDGEMENTS

Angela Hoover, rights and reproductions manager, was a tremendous help getting images from the massive collection of historic images at the Chicago History Museum, which I've visited often to gaze at the dioramas that introduced me to Chicago's rich history and which I will always refer to as the Chicago Historical Society.

Rick Kogan of the *Chicago Tribune* for his supportive e-mails.

Joseph Pucci for sticking with me throughout the project.

Richard Rott and the gang of database enhancers who worked nights, weekends and holidays putting the *Chicago Tribune* online.

INTRODUCTION

On a mild morning in August 1907, hundreds of criminals, politicians and businessmen squeezed into a Catholic church on Chicago's West Side, sitting beside a group of pallbearers that included Chicago fire chief James Horan and a notorious gambler named Charley Winship. The men sat quietly, lost in their own thoughts, as four priests celebrated a solemn mass before an altar crammed with outlandishly large floral arrangements. Perhaps disgraced police superintendent William McGarigle remembered when McDonald used to pay him to overlook certain goings-on in McDonald's illegal gambling parlor. Perhaps "Oyster Joe" Chesterfield Mackin (inventor of the free lunch—a fork and an oyster, devised to entice customers to linger at his saloon) remembered rounding up drunken voters on election day and delivering them to McDonald's very own polling place in full view of McDonald's neighbor, Mayor Carter Harrison. Perhaps James Henry Farrell, leader of the Cook County Democratic Marching Club, remembered when Mike McDonald treated him and two hundred other Democrats to an all-expenses-paid excursion to Niagara Falls, a trip to celebrate the acquittal of an elected official charged with bribery.

Outside the church, police officers struggled to prevent throngs of onlookers from entering. Some of those same policemen would work overtime that day investigating an explosion at a gambling parlor owned by James O'Leary, an up-and-coming protégé of McDonald's and son of the famous Mrs. O'Leary, whose cow allegedly kicked over a lantern that started the Great Fire of 1871.

As Father Dorney prepared to deliver his eulogy, he nodded at members of McDonald's family assembled in the front row: his brother, his sister, his sons and his first wife, Mary. McDonald's current wife, Dora, was not among the mourners. The priest cleared his throat and began:

Ask Lyman J. Gage, great factor in one of the largest financial institutions in Chicago—he may be here, for aught I know—for his estimate of Mike McDonald. Doubtless he will tell you that Mike's paper and his word were good. Who was instrumental in placing Murray F. Tuley in the common council of the City of Chicago? Mike McDonald! Who subsequently had a great share in placing Murray F. Tuley on the bench? Who placed the other great jurist, McAllister, on the bench? Mike McDonald. [In exchange for securing the position, Judge McAllister declared a raid on Mike's gambling parlor illegal.]

Who was it that gave to the City of Chicago one of its best health commissioners and at a time when Chicago needed a big man for the position? I refer to Dr. Wickersham. Mike McDonald! [During the Civil War, Wickersham was accused of plotting to disrupt the 1864 Democratic Convention and free eight thousand Confederate prisoners from Camp Douglas on Chicago's South Side.]

Who was it they called the king of the politicians and the gamblers, but who was it whose shrewdness enabled him to exercise such a power? Mike McDonald!

He associated with gamblers and others without the pale of the church and gave scandal in various ways, but before his death he was heartily sorry for it, and he died a true Christian.

THE KID AND THE CANDY

Thirteen-year-old Michael Cassius McDonald ran away from home aboard a train headed to Chicago, tagging along with a gang of young ruffians from Upstate New York; one boy died under mysterious circumstances and was buried in Chicago by McDonald and the others. Such was the inauspicious start to McDonald's life in gritty Chicago.

McDonald's immigrant parents, Edward and Mary, worked hard and remained poor in one of the world's most impressive natural settings, Niagara Falls, celebrated for its fierce beauty as early as the seventeenth century. A nice place to visit, but Michael didn't want to live there. In 1683, European explorer Father Louis Hennepin published the first written description of Niagara Falls in his book *Nouvelle Decouverte d'un Tres Grand Pays Situé Dans l'Amerique*:

> *Betwixt the Lake Ontario and Erie, there is a vast and prodigious Cadence of Water which falls down after a surprising and astonishing manner, insomuch that the Universe does not afford its parallel…four leagues from Lake Frontenac there is an incredible Cataract of water-fall which has no equal. At the foot of this horrible Precipice, we meet with the River Niagara.….It is so rapid above this Descent, that it violently hurries down the wild Beasts while endeavouring to pass it to feed on the other side, they not being able to withstand the force of its Current, which inevitably casts them above Six hundred foot high.*

Michael Cassius McDonald was born in an Irish enclave near Niagara Falls. *Library of Congress, cph3a21641//hdl.loc.gov/loc.pnp.chp3a21641.*

As the site was a thriving tourist destination, one tourist claimed that he could "hardly consent to leave this seemingly dangerous and enchanting spot." In December 1803, Niagara Falls welcomed its first honeymoon couple: Napoleon Bonaparte's younger brother Jerome and his bride, Betsy. Madly in love with each other despite warnings from both families that the marriage wouldn't last, the future king of Westphalia and the Baltimore socialite honeymooned in Niagara Falls. Perhaps Betsy Patterson Bonaparte packed sensibly for the chilly trip north, stuffing a few furs in her suitcases with her favorite dress—a dress so small that an acquaintance observed "it would easily fit into a gentleman's pocket." By all accounts, the honeymoon was a success, as a child was conceived, but the marriage was a failure. Jerome Bonaparte abandoned his American-born wife and child to marry Catharina of Wurttemberg.

The fierce Niagara River provided food and fur to the French and Native Americans in the seventeenth century; powered the sawmills, flour mills and paper mills where Irish immigrants toiled; and before the close of the nineteenth century generated hydroelectric power strong enough to light up Buffalo more than twenty miles away, due to the genius of Serbian immigrant Nikola Tesla.

Michael McDonald's father, Edward, fled County Cork, Ireland, as a stowaway bound for Canada. McDonald worked his way as a laborer through Quebec Province, where the seigneurial system of land distribution was just as unfavorable to the Irish as were the aristocratic English landlords who dominated the Irish in Ireland. He arrived in New York State too late to join the rush of Irish immigrants who built the nearby Erie Canal. Not that digging in muddy, disease-infested trenches would have appealed to Edward, yet many of his countrymen worked twelve to fifteen hours per day six days a week for meager meals, a small allowance of liquor and eighty cents per day, from which the cost of ticket from Ireland was deducted. At least in Niagara, New York, poor Irish immigrants received some relief, but only virtuous souls need apply:

> *No relief be given to persons known to be in possession of money exceeding in amount $5 nor to any person who shall refuse to work when wages considered reasonable by the Board are offered them, nor to any person who shall have been seen to beg from the inhabitants of the town, nor to any person who shall have been seen in a state of intoxication while receiving relief.*

In Niagara Edward McDonald wed Limerick-born Miss Mary Guy, a religious woman who bore him three children: Michael, Mary and the youngest, Edward Jr. The family lived in an Irish enclave where the women tried to keep their homes clean amid the stench and pollution of the paper mills that employed their husbands. They socialized at shops where they bought meat scraps and cabbage and prepared hot and nourishing, though not necessarily tasty, meals for the family dinner at the end of the day.

On Sundays, the McDonald family, usually without papa, attended mass at St. Raphael Roman Catholic Church. Mary, who was functionally illiterate, insisted that her brood attend mass on Sunday and parochial school during the week. Edward, a strict disciplinarian, regularly administered beatings to his children for disobedience, laziness and truancy. Unable to handle Michael, who preferred to spend his days learning practical math playing cards down at the railyard with fellow miscreants to staring out a classroom window, Edward "sold" Mike as an apprentice to a bootmaker. But Michael Cassius McDonald had his own plans for a future, plans that didn't include his father, boots or life in Niagara Falls. The restless boy found a job aboard trains headed to Chicago, selling candy and newspapers to passengers during the day and sleeping in Chicago's desolate railroad yards at night.

In the 1850s, travel by train was quicker than riding a horse, walking on dirt paths or bouncing along in a wagon, but sitting on a rough wooden plank in a stifling railroad car was just as uncomfortable as any horse or wagon that crossed the prairie. In winter, passengers huddled around potbellied stoves that, on occasion, set their clothing on fire. Summer weather meant that passengers could open windows, but along with "fresh air" came dust, cinders, bugs and thick black soot that covered passengers, who emerged as though traveling in a coal mine. Amenities such as carpeted aisles, upholstered chairs and dining cars staffed by attentive waiters didn't appear until 1865, when Chicagoan George Pullman sold the railroads his eponymous traveling coaches. Passengers brought their own food or relied on the meager, stale fare hawked by vendors at train stations or candy sold by boys like Michael McDonald.

Every day, hundreds of trains deposited thousands of passengers in Chicago. Some came for business and others for pleasure. Railroads played a part in Chicago's economic growth more than in any other city. What began in the 1830s as a fur trading post on Lake Michigan developed into an economic powerhouse because of railroads, which brought bright-eyed entrepreneurs from New England and transported goods manufactured in Chicago back to heavily populated eastern states. U.S. Senator Stephen A. Douglas (of the famous Lincoln/Douglas debates) championed the construction of Chicago's railroad system for both political and personal reasons. (Long-distance passengers inconvenienced by the necessity of changing trains at Chicago's Union Station can blame Stephen Douglas.) He recognized the need for a railroad to transport grain from millions of acres of untapped farmland in the West to growing populations in New York City and Boston. Deliberations to designate a city as the nation's railroad hub came to a head at a national railroad conference in 1849. The conference board favored cities with a temperate climate—cities such as St. Louis, Memphis and New Orleans—but the influential Chicagoan was determined that trains would terminate in Chicago, where, not so coincidentally, he had purchased a great deal of land along railroad tracks, speculating its value would increase. To facilitate the plan, Senator Douglas sponsored the Kansas-Nebraska Act, which opened land west of Missouri to American settlers and incidentally set the stage for the Civil War by allowing settlers in these new territories to decide the issue of slavery.

When Douglas shrewdly donated ten acres of land to a group of Baptists that established what would become the University of Chicago, the value of his adjacent land skyrocketed. But Stephen Douglas did not live long enough to enjoy his newly purchased real estate, as he died of typhoid fever two months after the attack on Fort Sumter and was buried on his never-completed estate in the neighborhood now

Senator Stephen A. Douglas brought railroad lines to Chicago. *Library of Congress, cph3a05504/hdl. loc.gov/loc.pnp.cph.3a05504.*

known as Bronzeville. His heirs donated forty-two acres of land to the Union army for training new recruits, but by 1863, the new Camp Douglas had been converted into a notorious prison where four thousand Confederate soldiers died under harsh conditions and were buried in a cemetery on Sixty-Seventh Street. It was during the Camp Douglas years that Michael McDonald began a career as a war profiteer.

As the trains tugged and jerked along the rails, young Mike walked through the coaches selling candy and newspapers to passengers bored of an unchanging landscape seen through dirty windows. Always clever, Mike carefully refolded discarded newspapers and sold the same newspapers again and again to passengers who hopped aboard along the way to Chicago. Of course, it took a good salesman to sell the first candy box and an even better salesman to make the second, third and fourth sales. Just as he had recycled his newspapers to unsuspecting passengers, he carefully repacked and tidied up his candy boxes.

There were plenty of gullible passengers—as Michael Cassius McDonald said half a century before P.T. Barnum, "There's a sucker born every minute."

"Wouldn't you like a box of candy for the lovely lady?" he'd ask a well-dressed man while he smiled at the man's wife, mistress or sister. Or he'd grab an empty seat near a solitary man and strike up a conversation, listen to his story and propose a box of candy as the answer to anything. A man could celebrate a triumphant business deal or ease the pain of disappointment with a box of candy. But selling candy was kid's stuff.

Early on, Michael McDonald invented the "prize package scam," a con game popularized twenty years later in the Wild West by Jefferson Randolph "Soapy" Smith, the father of Denver's organized crime syndicate. Practiced around the world even today, especially in places where tourists with time on their hands and money in their pockets think that they are smarter than the local population, the game offers a cash prize in every package. Soapy stuffed $100 bills in packages of soap and then planted an accomplice in the audience who bought the lucky soap and returned the prize to Soapy. In the beginning, McDonald couldn't afford to offer more than a $5 prize.

Amy Reading, author of *The Mark Inside: A Perfect Swindle, a Cunning Revenge and a Small History*, wrote, "At a young age, McDonald left home to ride the rails as a train butcher, someone who peddled newspapers, candy and other comforts to weary travelers, hustling tips and meals. McDonald added to his income with a short con of his own invention, the prize package swindle. He'd flamboyantly insert $5 bills in several of the candy boxes in his cart and tell passengers that every box held a prize ranging from one penny to $5." Passengers ripped through box after box, barely noticing its stale, squashed contents, until their hopes were dashed or they ran out of money. Occasionally, to show that the swindle was honest, he allowed a passenger to win a five-dollar bill.

Even at a young age, Mike knew that his future was in gambling. He played well, and he learned to read his opponent's face. So, the teenager dropped the brogue he had developed living in Niagara's Irish enclave and affected the mannerisms of a successful businessmen. He bought fine clothes and smoked cigars to appear older. On board, he played cards with passengers twice his age who accepted him into their circle and treated him like an equal. Soon he rarely spent time with the other boys, who were happy to earn a few cents for each newspaper or box of candy they sold. While the other boys sought shelter in any dry, though not necessarily clean, structure waiting for a train back to New York, Mike spent his evenings playing cards in a Chicago firehouse near the station.

The bright young man might have chosen a legitimate occupation in any town along the train route or even traveled west to stake a claim in the newly opened territories, but Chicago's reputation as a wide-open city beckoned to him. He felt comfortable with Irish immigrants, who accounted for one-fifth of the population of Chicago. Never mind that frequent epidemics of cholera, dysentery, scarlet fever and smallpox resulted in the deaths of thousands of citizens. What did it matter to a healthy, invincible teenager? Besides, the city was working to solve its health issues by raising buildings above the muddy quagmire that harbored nasty microbes. Newly laid sewers would carry polluted water from buildings downtown into Lake Michigan. The most remarkable example happened when George Pullman, future inventor of the eponymous Pullman Palace train car, lifted the Tremont Hotel six feet without disturbing the guests inside, a feat celebrated by the *Chicago Tribune*: "Nothing better illustrates the energy and determination with which the makes of Chicago set about a task when once they had made up their minds, than the speed and thoroughness with which they solved the problem of the city's drainage and sewage."

When Michael Cassius McDonald settled in the city, Chicago tolerated all manner of vice—prostitution, gambling and drunkenness—and did little to enforce morals laws. Although the city built a jail when it incorporated in 1833, it didn't establish a police force until the mid-1850s and didn't provide officers with uniforms until three years later. When Chicago mayor Levi Boone, nephew of frontiersman Daniel Boone, tried to enforce a law that prohibited the sale of liquor on Sundays, the city erupted into riots.

Boone's successor, "Long John" Wentworth, condemned the police force in his inaugural address:

> *Our police system has been gradually falling into disrepute; and it is a lamentable fact that, whilst our citizens are heavily taxed to support a large police force, a highly respectable private police* [the Pinkerton Detective Agency on Washington Street, led by the world's original private eye, Allan Pinkerton] *is doing a lucrative business. Our citizens have ceased to look to the public police for protection, for the detection of culprits or the recovery of stolen property. It cannot be relied upon for the preservation of order, as was evinced on the day of our recent election.*

Newspapers printed stories of abysmal police work. For example, in a period of only a few weeks, reporters wrote about the absence of police on election day. When fights broke out all over the city, a crowd of 1,500 drunks attempted to influence voters entering a polling place by beating them with their fists; a crowd kicked an innocent bystander in the head, yelling, "Kill him, kill him!" until his friends intervened; an out-of-town guest in a fine hotel paid the police a fifty-dollar reward, plus expenses, for the return of his stolen watch; a father offered a reward to find the driver of a buggy who ran over his young daughter because the police officer who witnessed the crime refused to intervene; and a group of police officers chided a victim for falling prey to a pickpocket.

Fed up with crime, Mayor Wentworth—an intimidating man who stood six-foot-six, weighed more than three hundred pounds and ate thirty-course meals washed down with a pint of whiskey—took matters into his own hands to destroy Chicago's vice district on April 27, 1857. For years, prostitutes, pimps, hustlers and thieves had operated without interference from police officers, some of whom would not enter the vice district known as "The Sands" under any circumstances. Living in run-down shanties near Lake Michigan were characters like John and Mary Hill, a married couple who worked together. Mary entertained her customer while John watched through a hole in the wall until it was time to steal the naked man's clothing and wallet. Near the couple's shack lived Margaret McGuiness, a prostitute who boasted that she had not been sober for five years straight and had not worn clothes for three years, and Freddy Webster, the pimp who supplied her with forty men per night.

Knowing that folks who lived in The Sands couldn't resist temptation, Mayor Wentworth placed ads around town for a high-stakes dogfight on the outskirts of the city. While the scoundrels traveled to the bogus dogfight, Mayor Wentworth led a posse of thirty men, equipped with teams of horses, wagons and chains, and with brute force demolished much of The Sands. Buildings that didn't collapse were burned to the ground as crowds watched. With tacit permission from Mayor Wentworth, bystanders carried away anything they could carry.

The *Chicago Tribune* crowed: "Thus, this congregation of the vilest haunts of the most depraved and degraded creatures in our city, has been literally

'wiped out,' and the miserable beings who swarmed there, driven away. Hereafter we hope the Sands will be the abode of the honest and the industrious and that efficient measures will be taken to prevent any other portion of the city from becoming the abode of another such gathering of vile and vicious persons." Some of Chicago's most expensive real estate sits atop the land formerly known as The Sands.

But by demolishing The Sands, Wentworth dispersed crime to other sections of Chicago, making it easier for Mike McDonald to establish his gambling empire. Troy Taylor, author of *Murder and Mayhem in Chicago's Vice Districts*, wrote, "Wentworth's plan to clean up vice in Chicago backfired. Once the Sands was destroyed, the gamblers, criminals and whores who called the place home simply crossed the Chicago River and, instead of being mostly confined to one small area, spread throughout the city."

A reporter for the *Chicago Journal* wrote, "We are beset on every side by a gang of desperate villains."

Other decisions by Wentworth made citizens scratch their heads and question his competence as mayor, such as when he fired the entire police force, leaving the city without protection for days. When the uncommonly tall Wentworth grew tired of banging his head on signs that hung from stores above sidewalks, he declared the signs illegal, ordered them removed and burned them in a pile on a street downtown.

As vice districts popped up around Chicago, editors of the *Chicago Tribune*, a nativist Republican newspaper, declared that Irish immigrants, German immigrants and the Democratic Party were responsible for citywide gambling and drunkenness:

> *The great mass of the drinking and gambling population are identified in their political action, with the Democratic party.... The Irish vote alone, in Chicago, is greater than all the democratic majority, and with here and there*

Mayor Wentworth destroyed the vice district near Lake Michigan and the Chicago River. His actions allowed gambling to spread citywide—perfect for young Michael McDonald. *Library of Congress, ppmsca23149//hdl.loc. gov/ppmsca23149.*

a rare exception, it affiliates with the Democratic party....If the ignorant Catholic [Irish] and Sabbath-breaking Germans that haunt the saloons, gambling houses, and dens of shame, with which the city abounds...if all these were likewise drawn from the Democratic party, it would not number one thousand votes, out of six thousand, in the whole city.

Also from the *Chicago Tribune*:

In several places nearly whole blocks are occupied and used by both males and females, and are doubtless hotbeds, prolific of drunkenness, profanity, gambling and licentiousness...where time is wasted, morals destroyed, and the ignorant and unwary are robbed of their last dollar. That these places are nuisance to be abated by law....Our city officers should be encouraged to execute the laws and ordinances, to the very letter against unlicensed sabbath-breaking dram shops and against gambling establishments.

As gambling flourished in Chicago, McDonald amassed a small fortune playing a popular card game known as faro in illegal gambling parlors south of the Chicago River, mostly dirty and dark hovels but a few with deep carpets and elegantly upholstered furniture. *New York Times* bestselling author Win Blevins described the once immensely popular card game in *Dictionary of the West*: "A gambling game played with cards and popular in the West of the nineteenth century. In faro, the players bet on the order in which the cards will be turned over by the dealer....The name is said to come from the French word for pharaoh."

Michael McDonald could have invested his small fortune in Chicago's burgeoning real estate market and become very wealthy, but on a misguided impulse, the restless young man decided to try his luck in the Deep South. In the winter of 1860, Michael McDonald moved to New Orleans, where anything was possible. McDonald watched as politicians mingled with crowds of petty criminals in the city's five hundred illegal gambling parlors. Plantation owners openly bet on cockfights. Whores dressed in their finest frocks attended horseraces, and every night riverboats filled with gamblers floated along the unregulated water of the muddy Mississippi.

Once again McDonald changed his appearance. He got rid of his business suits and adopted the dress of a flashy card sharp fresh off the riverboat: burgundy brocade vest, gold pocket watch, wide-brimmed plantation owner's hat and a long frock coat. No pictures of McDonald as a riverboat gambler exist, but he must have been quite a sight, as he was the inspiration for riverboat gambler Gaylord Ravenal, the character created by his Chicago neighbor Edna Ferber for her novel *Showboat*.

McDonald's New Orleans adventure came to an immediate halt with the start of the Civil War. After April 12, 1861, Yankees were no longer welcome in the South. He barely escaped with his life by telling authorities that he voted for proslavery candidate Stephen Douglas, not Abraham Lincoln. In truth, McDonald's name did not appear on any voter registration documents at the time. McDonald packed his gear and boarded a steamer headed north. With plenty of time to think as he made the slow journey to Chicago, he developed a business plan. In *The Mark Inside*, Amy Reading called McDonald's plan "a recipe for vice that would prove enduring: separate gambling from prostitution, further separate brace games or rigged house games, from honest gentlemen's gaming, centralize interests, and pay regularly and handsomely for protection from police raids."

His future lay ahead in Chicago.

MICHAEL McDONALD THE WAR PROFITEER

Michael Cassius McDonald returned to Chicago during the early days of the Civil War to find that the city had changed. Its location far from the battlefields meant safety. Assured that day-to-day business would continue uninterrupted, Chicago's economy more than tripled supplying the Union army during the Civil War. Its many railway lines transported troops and goods to battlefields in the South. New banks opened to accept huge amounts of federal money sent to Chicago to buy supplies. Chicago's immigrant population worked hard to provide the military with much-needed uniforms, meat, grain, weapons, tents, horses, surgical equipment (e.g., long sharp knives and hack saws) and opium to dull the pain as a doctor amputated a soldier's limb, as well as, of course, lots of ammunition.

In their book *Civil War Chicago: Eyewitness to History*, authors Theodore J. Karamanski and Eileen M. McMahon described how the Civil War changed the fortunes of one small manufacturer: "Within two weeks after the firing on Fort Sumter, the War Department turned to Chicago Lead Works for bullets. Chicagoans were happy to deliver them to Southerners....[The owner] received at special commission from the State to furnish...10,000 lbs. of one-ounce balls and 2,000 the size for their army pistols."

In the spring of 1861 Gilbert, Hubbard & Company placed a small notice in a newspaper advertising its new supply of sacks made of hemp fiber. By autumn, the *Chicago Tribune* was congratulating the firm on the growth of its workforce and the fine products it manufactured for the government:

> *Since the outbreak of the war, this firm have enlarged their establishment directed their attention to the manufacture of tents, flags, regimental colors, and other concomitants of the camp....In the third* [floor], *a large force of men is employed in the manufacture of sails and other vessel appurtenances. In the fourth, a hundred sewing machines driven by steam and presided over by as many girls, fill the room with deafening clatter....Government is fast learning the fact that it is poor economy to ship articles of camp equipage from the East to the West, when they can be manufactured at such low rates in Chicago.*

The military needed to feed its hungry men, and Chicago stepped up to the plate as it were. Cincinnati, the self-proclaimed "Porkopolis," lost its place as America's largest pork processor when the war cut off the city's supply of pigs from Southern states, setting the stage for Chicago to don the crown, processing more than 500,000 hogs in a single year. Farmers in Iowa and Kansas loaded their cattle onto railroad cars bound for Chicago slaughterhouses (consolidated as the Union Stockyards in1865), which processed more than 80 percent of the nation's beef. Chicago even took over processing the South's most iconic crop: sorghum. Enterprising farmers in Southern Illinois shipped their new crops to what is now the trendy West Loop neighborhood, where the West Side Sorghum Refinery converted the grain to sweet, sticky syrup. Chicago fed thousands of Confederate soldiers imprisoned in Camp Douglas on Chicago's South Side, and in the long-standing Chicago tradition of patronage, President Abraham Lincoln gave the job of procuring meat for the camp to his brother-in-law, Ninian Wirt Edwards. As commissary of subsistence for Illinois, Edwards contracted with suppliers of poor-quality meat, resulting in embarrassment for the president, malnourishment of prisoners and an investigation of Edwards for fraud.

Michael McDonald settled down in Bridgeport, a predominantly Irish American neighborhood on Chicago's South Side, originally settled by a small group of impoverished Irish immigrants who came to Chicago to escape discrimination and famine. Their numbers reached twenty thousand in the 1860s. Most families lived in small wooden structures that newspapers described as "squalid shanties," occupied by "wild and drunken Irishmen." Bound by a common religion, the Irish attended mass at Catholic churches,

heeded the advice of parish priests and socialized with like-minded folks at church functions. Whether McDonald belonged to any parishes is not known, but no doubt he felt at home in Bridgeport, with its fierce identity as an Irish neighborhood; no doubt he enjoyed Bridgeport's easy access to illegal gambling parlors in downtown Chicago.

No battles were fought in Chicago, but thousands of its citizens fought battles in the Southern states. After the attack at Fort Sumter, President Lincoln issued a call for seventy-five thousand volunteers from Northern states, including six thousand from Illinois. Regiments filled quickly with Chicago's unskilled Irish immigrants, who sought a signing bonus, a steady paycheck and freedom from discrimination. By the end of the war, more than fifteen thousand Chicagoans had served in the Union army, four thousand of whom died on the battlefields of the South.

Some Irish Catholics in Illinois heeded the impassioned plea of a local priest to give back to their adopted country:

> *I wish every man who can leave his family, to enlist. This is the first country the Irishman ever had that he could call his own country. The flag of the stars and stripes is the only flag he can fights under and defend as his own flag. No, in the time of the nation's peril, let every Irishman show that he is worthy to be part of a great and glorious nation. Now, when the American flag is bombarded and struck down by traitors, let every Irishman show that he is true to the flag which always protects him. I want every Irishman who hears me to enlist if he can. There are two classes whom I must despise—cowards and traitors; and those who can enlist, and do not, are either one or the other.*

In the spring of 1861, notices on plastered on walls urged the Bridgeport Irish to join the Irish Brigade of the Union army: "Rally! All Irishmen in favor of forming a regiment of Irish volunteers to sustain the Government of the United States, in and through the resent war, will rally at North Market

During the Civil War, German and Irish immigrants added to Chicago's economy, providing meat to the Union army. The consolidation of several slaughterhouses resulted in the creation of the Union Stockyards. *Library of Congress, pan6a4140//hdl.loc.gov/loc.pnp/pan6a4140.*

Hall, this evening April 20th. Come all! For the honor of the old land rally for the defense of the new!"

The plea to form an Irish brigade was allegedly signed by James A. Mulligan, Alderman Comiskey, M.C. McDonald and other prominent members of Chicago's Irish American community. But pleas by the Catholic Church and an ethnic esprit de corps to join the Union army did not sway Michael Cassius McDonald. Some historians have questioned whether "M.C. McDonald" referred to Michael Cassius McDonald or another Mr. McDonald. In his biography of McDonald, *The Gambler King of Clark Street: Michael McDonald and the Rise of Chicago's Democratic Machine*, author Richard C. Lindberg wrote, "Crime historian Herbert Asbury and Chicago journalist Henry Justin Smith repeated [the] dubious assertion in their own published volumes, but the truth is McDonald did not return to Chicago until the fall of 1861. He signed no petitions, made no pledges or guarantees, and swore no oaths of allegiance to any particular cause, save his own."

After the initial burst of American pride diminished, the government couldn't find enough volunteers to fill the ranks of the Union army. To remedy the shortage of volunteers, the U.S. Congress enacted the Enrollment Act of 1863, which required every able-bodied male between the ages of twenty and forty-five to serve in the Union army. Every able-bodied male, that is, except the nation's men whose wealthy families could afford to pay the military a $300 fee or who could convince someone like a farmhand or a member of house staff to serve as a substitute.

Needless to say, the draft was not popular among the poor in Chicago. In Bridgeport, a crowd of more than three hundred men, women and children chased away federal officers looking for potential draftees, and in a report of a protest, the *Chicago Tribune* showed an obvious bias against the Irish:

The infuriated Irish…howling like demons…are a lawless, reckless class of the community, embracing the very lowest most ignorant, depraved and besotted rabble that can be found in the city.

McDonald's name erroneously appeared on a poster to join James A. Mulligan's Irish Brigade. *Library of Congress, cwpb06232, https://hdl.loc.gov./loc.pnp/cwpb.06232.*

There is but one class of people in this city who refuse to give their names to the enrolling officers—the Irish. They exhibit less loyalty than any other nationality....But the Irish throw all sorts of obstacles in the way. Many of them dodge and hide from the marshals, and when found they give false names and try to deceive the officer or mulishly refuse to answer....Frequently they beat or otherwise maltreat those who give their names to the officers. And in one case they collected a mob and assaulted the officers, nearly murdering them. Why do the Irish behave so badly? No class of people are more largely debtors to our free institutions.....No class of people are fonder of voting or holding office or sharing the good things that Freedom scatters among her votaries. Why, then should they hesitate to defend the Government and the institutions which have conferred upon them so many blessings? Their conduct is basely ungrateful, and the stigma they are fixing upon themselves will take many a year to obliterate. If the Irish intend to resist the draft and refuse to fight for the Union, what right have they to vote or hold office? The Irish should make up their minds to obey the laws, and contribute their equitable share to the National defence, as do the Germans and other nationalities....Is it not the bound duty of every intelligent Irishman to use his influence with his more illiterate countrymen, to open their eyes and instruct them in the obligations of patriotism and good citizenship?

When the secretary of war issued an order prohibiting eligible men from leaving the United States without the expressed consent of the federal government, a Chicago newspaper accused several hundred Irish Americans, including Michael McDonald, of claiming Irish or Canadian citizenship to avoid the draft. Federal agents who patrolled Chicago's many train stations offered Chicago policemen a five-dollar reward for each eligible draftee they found, but many neighborhood policemen refused to participate.

This widespread prejudice toward the Irish and Irish Americans is not borne out by statistics compiled in 1869 by the federal government in its publication *Investigations in the Military and Anthropological Statistics of American Soldier*, which notes that 150,000 Irish and Irish American served in the Civil War.

Finally, to sweeten the prospect of dying or returning home severely maimed, the military offered a signing bonus, known as a "bounty." The authors of *Civil War Chicago: Eyewitness to History* explain how bounty bonuses were paid in Chicago: "The bonus system offered positive inducements to patriotic service. Although the State of Illinois did not offer a bonus, the

City of Chicago and most of the city's wards did offer cash incentives which amounted to several hundred dollars—a tidy sum when working men earned a dollar a day for hard physical labor." The bonus led to the emergence of a new wartime occupation: bounty jumper. Chicago became the Midwest center for men who enlisted to collect a bonus and then immediately deserted.

McDonald's experience dodging bullets on his journey back to Chicago soured him on joining the military. The signing bonus was tempting, but why risk being hanged as a deserter? Why not get others to sign up and collect their bounties? It was as a "bounty broker" that McDonald organized his first crime syndicate, employing his fellow gamblers to find derelicts to enlist in the Union army, sometimes enlisting the same men several times. McDonald's brokerage rounded up men so drunk or mentally addled that they had trouble signing their own name, or any name, to enlistment papers. He paid the gamblers a finder's fee and pocketed the rest of the signing bonus. No doubt some of the hundreds of men who drunkenly signed enlistments papers and then fled were hanged, but McDonald was never charged with a crime. And while McDonald and his men dominated the Midwest, a German immigrant named Adam Worth controlled the East Coast. Worth enlisted in the Union army when he was seventeen and was injured in the Second Battle of Bull Run. While recovering from his wounds at the Washington, D.C., hospital, he discovered he was listed as killed in action, so he enlisted again under an alias and collected a bounty. After enlisting in both the Union army and the Confederate army numerous times, he established his own bounty brokerage similar to McDonald's.

When the Civil War ended and there were no more bounties to collect, Adam Worth moved to London, where he organized a band of thieves and became known as the "Napoleon of Criminals" due to his short stature. His crimes and keen intellect so impressed author Sir Arthur Conan Doyle that he used Worth as a model for criminal mastermind James Moriarty, archenemy of Sherlock Holmes. In 1876, Mr. Worth stole Thomas Gainsborough's *Portrait of Georgiana, the Duchess of Devonshire*, one of the most valuable paintings in England, and kept it hidden for twenty-five years until he brought the painting to Chicago's Pinkerton Agency on Washington Street, where he exchanged it for immunity from his crimes.

With no signing bonuses to collect, Michael McDonald opened a bar and a small gambling parlor in the Richmond Hotel, formerly a grand hotel that honored guests such as the Prince of Wales. Here McDonald provided a place where working men could spend their disposable income.

Gainfully employed as meatpackers and factory workers in postwar Chicago, immigrants could pay rent, feed and clothe their families and have a little left over to spend on drinks and gambling. To grow the business, McDonald organized a ring of gamblers to lure travelers from the nearby train station into the bar, where he set up faro tables attractively decorated with tigers, the symbol of the faro card game. He paid protection money to police officers he knew from his Civil War days and schmoozed with politicians headed to city hall. With his success came a change in residence. Throughout the Civil War, Mike lived in Bridgeport with his cantankerous widowed father, but after the war, Mike left Bridgeport for a home in an upscale neighborhood better suited to impress his new lover, Belle Jewel, a chorus girl who danced at the McVicker's Theatre. Mike enjoyed showing off the beautiful woman at fine restaurants and charity balls. The inseparable couple lived together for seven years, and although they never married, McDonald considered Belle Jewel to be his wife.

LUCKY AT CARDS, UNLUCKY IN LOVE

By all accounts, Michael Cassius McDonald enjoyed a good life as a rich young man in Chicago. He gained a reputation as Chicago's most famous gambler, and every night he returned to his posh house on the city's South Side, where his "wife," Belle Jewel, the most beautiful chorus girl in Chicago, waited for him to return. But all that changed in the fall of 1871. Without explanation, Belle Jewel vanished from Chicago. No longer was the couple seen around town dining on quail and lemon cake at John Wright's restaurant in Crosby's Opera House or politely sipping fine cognac at Chapin & Gore after taking in a show at the McVicker's Theatre, where Belle had danced before meeting McDonald. He remained silent on the disappearance of his common-law wife, and it was not revealed until after his death that the lovely Ms. Jewel fled Chicago to join a St. Louis convent, where she died twenty years later.

In October 1871, the Chicago fire raged for three days, leaving in its path 100,000 homeless, 300 dead and more than 17,500 buildings burned to the ground. Churches, stores, hotels, theaters, schools, public buildings (including city hall) and private homes caught fire and fell to ashes in minutes. In the panic, children became separated and cried out for their mothers and fathers. Residents rushed into their burning homes to retrieve whatever they could, some so weighted down with furniture that they could barely move and were trampled to death by the fleeing mob. Wealthy residents hired, at great expense, wagons to transport family members and furniture away from the flames.

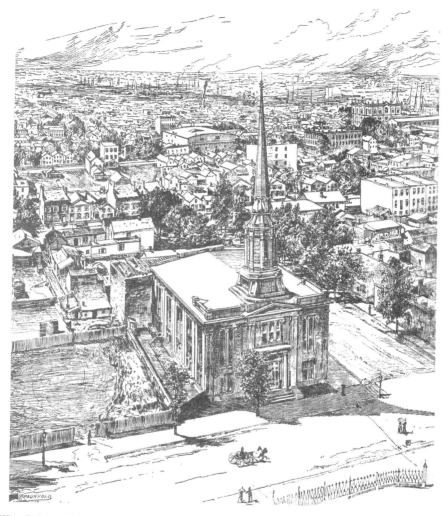

The Chicago Fire of 1871 destroyed more than seventeen thousand buildings, including city hall. *From* The History of Chicago *by A. T. Andreas.*

Newspapers around the world reported on the panic in Chicago as the fire raged. From the *Baltimore Sun*:

> *Wide-Spread Devastation—Scenes of Terror and Desolation—Great Loss of Life....The most terrible conflagration that ever occurred in this city broke out about 11 o'clock last night....The glare from the burning buildings lighted the streets half a mile away, so that one could see to*

read.…The flames are raging with increased fury in every direction, and God's mercy can only save the city from utter destruction. A fearful panic prevails all through the streets, where the people are rushing to and fro, and weeping and wailing.…The alarm-bell has just commenced ringing an unceasing peal, which is intended to call every sleeper from his bed. The panic is increasing, and the people seem almost crazy with alarm. The vessels in the river catching fire in every direction, and all in the South River will probably be destroyed. A raging, roaring hell of fire envelops the city…sweeping onward a whirlwind of flames against which human efforts are powerless.

The editor of the *Belfast News-Letter* received word when a White Star Line steamship reached Northern Ireland that martial law had been declared. It reported, "General Sheridan has complete control, and confidence is fully restored."

Although the deadly tragedy cost millions of dollars and hundreds of lives, the Chicago fire did not destroy Chicago in its entirety. The so-called Burnt District, as it became known, was bounded on the south from De Koven Street (former site of the O'Leary Barn and current site of the Chicago Fire Academy) north to Fullerton Avenue, east from Lake Michigan and west to the Chicago River.

Within a week, rumors had spread that Mrs. Catherine O'Leary's cow kicked over a lamp in the family barn, igniting a fire that devastated the city. Again the *Chicago Tribune* showed its distain for Bridgeport's Irish community by referring to Mrs. O'Leary as an "Irish Hag."

In testimony before the board of police, Catherine O'Leary told the board that she did not milk cows by lamplight and she was asleep in her home with her husband, Patrick, and their children and was awakened by the sound of a neighbor pounding on her door, alerting the family that the barn and several homes were on fire. When a member of the board of police asked why her house didn't burn down along with thousands of other buildings, she replied that there was a hydrant on each side of it, and a hundred of her friends filled buckets with water and threw them on the sides and roof of the building. Despite her denial, the O'Leary family was shunned by the general public. Son Jimmy turned to gambling, first and as a protégé of Michael McDonald and then as his rival when he opened a racetrack in Indiana that competed with McDonald's west side racetrack.

The rumor of the cow and the lantern gained steam in the twentieth century with a parody of the nineteenth-century minstrel song "There'll Be a Hot Time in the Old Town Tonight," adding the lyrics, "Late one night when we were all in bed, Old Mother Leary left her lantern in the shed. And when the cow kicked it over, she winked her eye and said: 'There'll be a hot time in the old town tonight!'" and ended in 1997, when Mrs. O'Leary and her cow were exonerated by Alderman Ed Burke, who stated in a Chicago City Council meeting, "Mrs. O'Leary and her cow are innocent of any blame for the fire that raged behind their house."

Within days of the fire, Chicago began to recover. Shops opened for business inside poorly constructed makeshift sheds selling goods salvaged from the ruins of the fire. Railroads filled with supplies donated by rival cities Milwaukee and St. Louis arrived daily. Foreign countries, including China, donated more than $900,000 to aid in the recovery. Rubble cleared and dumped into Lake Michigan created new, and soon to be pricy, real estate along Lake Michigan. And just as destruction of The Sands in 1857 didn't put an end to illegal gambling (instead allowing gambling parlors to proliferate), gambling flourished again after the Great Chicago Fire, as thousands of sightseers flocked to Chicago to witness firsthand the ruins and to have a little fun at Chicago's newest brothels and gambling parlors.

Within a few weeks, Mike McDonald began to recover. Although he lost all of his uninsured real estate and businesses, he managed to raise enough money to set up a saloon at State and Harrison that featured illegal card

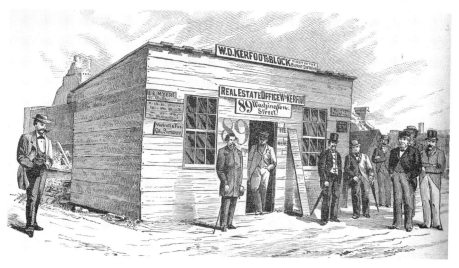

Following the Chicago fire, entrepreneurs opened businesses in makeshift sheds. *From* The History of Chicago *by A. T. Andreas.*

games, and by December, he had replaced his common-law wife with his first legal wife.

On December 5, 1871, Michael Cassius McDonald married Mary Ann Noonan in a Catholic church on Chicago's South Side. Like Mike, Mary was born to Irish Catholic immigrants in Upstate New York, and like Mike, she had been a troublesome teen. The family moved to a small town in Ohio, and at age fifteen, she married a local boy by the name of John Goudy; by age seventeen, she was a mother with two infants. After the birth of her second child, Mary developed an obsession with Catholicism and, in particular, its priests. (This obsession would eventually find its way into her marriage to Michael McDonald.) She prayed herself into a frenzy, probably at St. Mary's, a Catholic church in Tiffin, Ohio, built by Irish Immigrants. It was then that a priest, claiming to be a relative, invited the teenage mother of two on an excursion to Chicago, where she met McDonald, who was living with his common-law wife, Belle Jewel. Perhaps Mary and the priest made an innocent pilgrimage to some Catholic church—or perhaps not. The details of their meeting are not recorded, but Mike couldn't get the girl from Ohio out of his mind. When his relationship with Ms. Jewel ended, Mike married Mary Ann Noonan Goudy and adopted her two children.

Trouble began in the household almost immediately. Mary wasted no time to begin enjoying all that Chicago had to offer (theaters, fine restaurants and expensive shops), but she complained about being stuck at home with two children. She complained about living in the house once occupied by Mike and his former lover, although it was definitely a giant step up from the home she shared with her first husband in Ohio. She complained that Mike didn't pay her enough attention and paid too much attention to gambling—the profession that fed and clothed her and her two children. Mary resented her plight as a neglected housewife and confided to a relative her desire to leave for Europe with or without her husband and children. But some of her complaints were not without merit. Mike often drank heavily, and when he did, he beat Mary, sometimes brutally. Mary told the *Chicago Tribune*, "The trouble between my husband and me grew out of his brutality. He was a big, red-blooded man, but when under the influence of liquor, he was rough and disorderly. He often struck me at such times and mistreated me in other cruel ways."

As a gambler, his income was not steady, and on occasion even he, the great Michael Cassius McDonald, played a losing hand. Perhaps in retaliation for him not paying her enough attention, Mary asked family friend William Buckley, a police captain, to pull an inebriated Mike from a faro card game

Mike married Mary Ann Noonan Goudy, a divorcée with two children. *Chicago History Museum, DN-0005338.*

at the gambling parlor owned by the corpulent Watt Robbins. The *Chicago Tribune* trumpeted the misfortunes of the man they called the "boss gambler in this city":

> *The boss gambler in this city has been "Mike" McDonald. The name is familiar to the public because it has appeared almost daily in the newspapers for several years, and always in connection with some nefarious transaction by which he grew rich at the expense of numerable victims....In the days before the fire, McDonald used to boast that he "ran the town" and openly intimated that he had the police offers under his thumb....Men were robbed nightly in his dens.*
>
> *Did he not know that thousands had lost in his dens, and that the same fate awaited his ill-gotten gains?...The gamblers say he lost $2,700, but the police were informed that he lost $6,000. Served him right....Fearing that the loss of so much money would drive him to intemperance and other recklessness, his wife, on Monday, applied to Capt. Buckley to assist her in reclaiming Michael. We are informed that Buckley sent a friend to Robbins' den, who upon stating his mission, was given to understand that Mrs. McDonald would be made to suffer for her nonsense when he caught her at home.*

By playing the hand she was dealt, Mary made a fool out of McDonald and gained the sympathy of many who considered him a thug, but McDonald would never be the adoring husband Mary wanted.

In September 1873, Mike McDonald moved Mary and the kids to an apartment above his new gambling parlor, which he called "The Store." It was a parlor the likes of which Chicago had never seen, a veritable department store of drinking and gambling open twenty-four hours a day. On the first floor, McDonald's staff sold fine imported cigars and the highest quality wine, as well as cheaper fare, both wholesale and retail. Customers in various stages of drunkenness were invited to gamble on the second floor, lavishly decorated with plush carpets that concealed trapdoors leading to hidden staircases, elaborate wallpaper with busy designs to hide peepholes and expertly hand-painted gambling tables. But he outfitted the family's living quarters above The Store with only basic furniture. Some of the family's spare rooms were reserved for "hotel guests" who needed a place to "lay low" for a while, either to avoid the police or to sleep off an alcohol-fueled night. Mary hated the situation, resenting every minute of her life with McDonald. Mary was now, in effect, the keeper of a boardinghouse, an occupation she had never imagined for herself. She cleaned and cooked for the family, but she drew the line at preparing meals for criminals. McDonald no longer stayed out all night at other haunts, but he risked the well-being of his wife and stepchildren by placing them so close to bar brawls, drunkenness and illegal gambling. On one occasion, the children witnessed the death of a hotel guest, a delirious yellow fever victim from the South who died in Mary's arms.

Once again, Mike put his skills as an organizer to good use as the operator of a crime syndicate. Men who ran illegal card games and other forms of gambling paid Mike a monthly protection fee to keep the police at bay. McDonald, of course, pocketed a portion of the group's contributions for himself and paid nothing from his own pocket for protection. McDonald, in turn, kept the police happy with cash and liquor, and when police officers were ordered to raid the gambling parlors, Mike was notified in advance and passed a heads-up along the grapevine to members of the organizations, who quickly stashed away cards and liquor. On occasion, the head of the police department ordered his men to destroy gambling equipment, so Mike brought in old furniture for the officers to chop to bits. McDonald's men carried the wooden chunks out onto the sidewalk, evidence that the police were legit, while the officers remained inside sipping expensive liquor.

Late one night, Mary awoke to the sound of intruders on the fire escape. Probably just a drunk looking for a spare room, she thought, but as a precaution, she grabbed "Pete," the twenty-inch revolver she kept nearby. Squinting in the darkness, she glimpsed three figures coming toward her. A man's voice announced that they were Chicago police officers with a warrant for the arrest of Michael McDonald. According the *Chicago Tribune*:

> [They] *informed her that they had a warrant for Mike McDonald, keeper of a gambling-house in that building, and demanded that she open the doors. She refused peremptorily, told the officers that she had been bothered altogether too much by policemen upon the same errand, and that the hotel of which she was manager was as reputable as any in the city, and therefore entitled to as much protection. She ended by ordering them out of the hall, that the rooms they wanted opened for their inspection were occupied by guests of the hotel who were entitled to all the protection due private individuals in their own domiciles.... [Mrs. McDonald] warned them from the head of the stairway that they were encroaching upon her private apartments—the home of herself and children. The officers say that she repeatedly ordered them out, but they considered that the warrant was sufficient, and they went ahead.*

Mary advanced toward the figures for a closer look and grew suspicious when she recognized one of the three men—not as a police officer, but as a man who knocked on her door earlier asking for a room to rent. With the twenty-inch revolver in hand, she warned the men not to take one step closer. When they advanced, she fired the gun.

"I've been shot!" yelled one of the officers. As Mary moved forward with the gun aimed directly at him, ready to fire again, he grabbed the gun and threw it to another officer. Mary McDonald was taken into custody and booked for assault with a deadly weapon with intent to kill; no charges were filed against Michael McDonald, and the arrest warrant carried by the injured police officer was not served.

Attorneys A.S. Trude and Emory Storrs argued for Mary's release on a writ of habeas corpus before a sympathetic judge in a courtroom packed with curious onlookers. Trude and Storrs would successfully defend the McDonalds several times throughout the course of their legal careers; although Trude remained loyal to the McDonald family, Storrs and McDonald had a failing out. When Storrs died in 1885, rumors circulated around the country that McDonald had poisoned him. From the *Austin American-Statesman*: "The story of the assassination of Emory A. Storrs, of Chicago, by putting digitalis in his whisky, is a startling fact, if true." McDonald claimed that Storrs drank himself to death and was never charged with the murder.

Storrs argued that the arrest warrant was fraudulently issued and that "under the circumstances, killing would have been justifiable." Judge McAllister agreed with Storrs and rebuked the city's police department, citing in his legal opinion their disregard for the "ancient maxim of common law that 'Every man's house is his castle…one of the sturdiest principles of Anglo-Saxon civil liberty,'" adding that in the city of Chicago "personal rights of the citizen are habitually disregarded, to my certain knowledge."

Charges against Mary McDonald were dropped, and the superintendent of police was not reappointed. Perhaps McDonald's friendship with Judge McAllister and members of the city council who voted not to reappoint the police superintendent played a part in these events. On another occasion, members of the demoralized police force did not bother to charge Mary McDonald with attempted murder when, armed with two revolvers, she savagely attacked a woman she had seen in the company of her husband.

Over the years, the relationship between McDonald and his wife became strained. He drank more, and when he drank, he beat her. Soon she began to spend her days at matinee performances to escape her world, if only for a few hours. New theaters built after the Great Fire offered everything

Above: Members of the Chicago City Council met here to consider Michael McDonald's suggestion to fire the police chief. *From* The History of Chicago *by A. T. Andreas.*

Left: Billy Arlington, a famous African American performer, had an affair with Mary McDonald while she was married to the gambler. *Harvard University Theatre Collection HTC, Hollis olvwork540378.*

under the sun: the McVicker's Theatre was a favorite venue for Shakespeare since the time President Abraham Lincoln's assassin, John Wilkes Booth, performed in *Richard III*; Russian pianist Anton Rubenstein appeared at Aiken's Theater; and Haverly's Theater introduced Chicagoans to Italian operas, too high-toned for Mary, who preferred minstrel shows at Hooley's, where she was soon a regular in the theater that the *Chicago Tribune* charitably described as "French" and with "a Parisian ingenuity." For weeks, she attended minstrel shows starring the famous Billy Arlington. Newspapers from Boston to Oakland raved about Arlington's performances as a minstrel; the *Ohio Statesman* called him "the best in the business." The *Buffalo Morning Express* wrote, "He is one of the best minstrel comedians extant." The *Sioux City Journal* noted, "The funniest man on the American stage." The African American man performed for white audiences in theaters around the country, where ladies and gentlemen rose from their seats and applauded him, but offstage Arlington faced racism, strangers called him "burnt cork" and he once was removed from a train by a white train conductor who overheard him joking with black Pullman porters. Tired of constant traveling away from his family, Arlington secured a long engagement at Hooley's Theatre, where management paid him a salary of $125 per week, enough to support his wife, Julia, and daughter, Amelia, in grand style on the city's South Side.

No doubt the handsome actor, whose real name was Valentine Burnell, noticed Mary McDonald sitting in the front row every Wednesday and Saturday. After all, some men thought her to be the prettiest girl in Chicago, but he did not initiate the relationship—not that he hadn't had extramarital affairs in the past. After a performance one day, Mary sent a note backstage inviting the actor to dine with her at Buckminster's Restaurant, considered by the *Chicago Tribune* to be a "high toned" establishment serving "sumptuous meals."

Within weeks they were an item. The pair wrote love letters; Mary signed hers under her pet name "Mamie" and Arlington signed his "Val." The couple met for secret trysts in Chicago's finest hotels while an oblivious Mike drank and gambled. When Arlington accepted a short engagement at an out-of-town venue, Mary concocted a scheme to spend a week alone with Arlington at McDonald's expense. Under the guise of visiting her mother, Mary took a train to Ohio, where she joined Arlington, never leaving their hotel room.

When Arlington accepted a three-month engagement in San Francisco, Mary invited herself to stay with him in California. She needed an alibi to cover her absence from home, so she complained to Mike that she needed a winter vacation in a warm climate. Her sympathetic husband listened as she explained that her health suffered during severe Chicago winters. Wouldn't a vacation in California be beneficial to her fragile condition? Couldn't he spare a few hundred dollars to cover her traveling expenses? Mike fell for her lies. With Mike's money in hand, she kissed her children goodbye and boarded a train for the long journey to San Francisco. Somewhere along the route, Mary impulsively telegraphed Mike, informing him their marriage was over—due, in a bizarre twist, to *his* infidelity. A baffled McDonald, who by all accounts had never been unfaithful, hired a team of private detectives who traced Billy Arlington and Mary to a hotel in San Francisco. Armed with this information, McDonald followed the pair to California.

No one knows for certain what happened between McDonald, his wife and her lover. Historian Jay Robert Nash wrote in his 1981 book *People to See: Anecdotal History of Chicago's Makers and Breakers*, "An enraged Big Mike tracked the pair to the Palace Hotel where, gun in hand, he intended to shoot them. McDonald's wife leaped between her avenging husband and her high-bouncing lover. Screamed Mary, 'Mike, for God's sake! Don't shoot! Take me back! For the love of God.'"

Historian Richard Lindberg wrote in his biography of McDonald that Mike had two pistols and that Mary screamed, "Mike, shoot me! I don't deserve to live." The *Sterling Daily Gazette* claimed that Mary got down on her knees, kissed a crucifix and swore on her children's souls that she had been faithful to Mike.

Billy Arlington shared his version of the events with the *San Francisco Chronicle* shortly after the encounter. He claimed that the two men cordially shook hands when they met and that neither man brandished a weapon. Billy had advised Mary to return home, generously offering to furnish the funds for that purpose if necessary. To this Mike replied, "Billy, my wife has told me all; I am to blame for her desertion." The reporter added that Billy "feels innocent of being the cause of all this trouble; and, if Mike McDonald would tell the truth, the bulk of the charges would fall to the ground." A few years later, Arlington retired from his career in minstrel shows, reinventing himself as a sort of a black Mark Twain, delivering humorous lectures around the country. He moved to Los Angeles with his wife and daughter, dying there in 1913. His death was reported in newspapers around the world.

Billy Arlington finished his San Francisco engagement, and the McDonalds boarded a train to Chicago. Somewhere along the way, Mary became troublingly unsettled. Lindberg reported that she aimed a pistol at

Mike, who calmed her with the promise to buy her anything she wanted if she would return to Chicago and resume her duties as a wife and mother.

What did she wish to have? A new hat? New furniture? No, Mary wanted a new house, a big house in a swanky neighborhood. So, Mike moved the family, including his father, Ed, whom Mary detested, to Ashland Boulevard, home to the stately residences of prominent citizens, including Mayor Carter Harrison. He outfitted the eighteen-room mansion with the finest furniture money could buy: Oriental carpets, his and hers busts carved from the finest marble, a grand piano and, for Mary to atone for her sins, a private chapel.

Mike supported his wife's renewed devotion to the Catholic Church with large contributions to the newly elevated Roman Catholic Archdiocese of Chicago. So, when Father Bergeron, a French Canadian priest, showed up at his house one day to solicit money for construction of a new a neighborhood church, Mike McDonald generously contributed. Although the family were members of St. Jarlath's, a South Side church with a large Irish American congregation, he furnished the priest with room and board during the three-year construction of the Romanesque-style Notre Dame de Chicago. Feeling generous, Mike told his wife, "If the priests down there [are] hungry bring them all up and feed them." No longer a regular theatergoer, Mary filled her empty afternoons at the construction site flirting with a young priest named Father Joseph Moysant, and with Mike's approval, she invited him to dine with the family. The priest soon became a regular at the McDonald family's dinner table. When he hinted that he needed somewhere to live as construction of the church continued, McDonald took him in temporarily. The priest stayed for two years.

The young priest taught Mike's younger children to recite their prayers and heard his wife's confession twice a week in the family's private chapel. The twenty-seven-year-old priest seemed harmless; he was, after all, a duly ordained priest whose appearance Mike described as "fat, French, greasy and lecherous." A fellow priest agreed with Mike, referring to Father Moysant as "a man of low breeding…raw boned, awkward, uncouth and about as handsome as a bull pup." But to Mary, Father Joseph Moysant was an Adonis. The forty-two-year-old mother of four (two still at home, two grown) and grandmother of two was smitten, beguiled, infatuated, love-struck and obsessed.

At Mike's expense, Father Moysant romanced Mary in Chicago's finest hotels: the Grand Pacific Hotel, the Palmer House and the Sherman House, as well as at the Waverly Hotel in Dixon, Illinois, when the priest temporarily transferred to a church downstate. The pair was discovered only once during

Mary McDonald had an affair with a Catholic priest while she was married to the gambler. Mary and her lover often shared a room at the Grand Pacific Hotel. *From* The History of Chicago *by A. T. Andreas.*

their two-year affair when a waitress who brought a pitcher of beer up to the couple's hotel room recognized Mary's so-called brother as the local priest.

Mike remained oblivious to the affair between his wife and Father Moysant, although the household staff viewed their closeness with suspicion—too many locked doors and too many lengthy "prayer sessions" in the family's private chapel. Father Moysant worried that if their affair became public, Mary might end the relationship. If Mary chose to cast him aside, he would be defrocked, unemployed and homeless. One evening, the priest led Mary into the chapel to cement their future forever. The *New York Times* reported, "Moysant induced Mrs. McDonald to consent to the performance of a marriage ceremony between them and officiated at the ceremony himself. Mrs. McDonald then swore upon a crucifix that she would regard nobody but Moysant as her husband."

Privately, Mary began to refer to herself as Mrs. Moysant, and shortly after the secret wedding, Mary took a trip to Tiffin, Ohio, with Mike's consent. Reflecting on the trip, McDonald told the *Rock Island Argus*:

She came to me about July 21 and told me she was going to Tiffin to find another grave for her father. Her father was buried there twenty-three years ago, but a street car line had been run through the cemetery and it was desirable to move his remains. She had been in the habit of visiting her mother at Tiffin, and I gave her $100. She said that was all she needed and declined to take any more money. [Mary returned a few days later to retrieve more money and jewelry worth $5,000.] *She started Wednesday. A day or so after she left I came home one night and was told Mrs. McDonald had come in in the garb of a Sister of Charity. I went up to see her and talked with her about it, and she said she had got through at Tiffin sooner than she expected, July 27, when I came home she had left.*

Curiously, McDonald didn't question why she had donned a nun's habit and blamed Moysant for her odd behavior:

The thieving, rascally fellow so worked upon the poor little woman that she did whatever he asked her to do. He got her to rob me, to take the money from my pocket at night, and in various ways made of our house all he could. He was a glutton—a hog—and would eat five meals a day and drink beer by the bucketful....I do not want to say anything against my wife. Spare her but give that lecherous wretch who calls himself a priest all the tortures of hell if possible. It may do very well for preachers to preach of eleventh-hour repentance, and all that kind of stuff, but if such men as that can go to heaven, I want to go plumb straight to hell when I die.

I have since found out [from the Pinkerton detectives he hired to track her down] *that she sailed from New York on the steamer La Normandie on July 29 in company with Father Moysant.*

When she went on shipboard she was dressed as a Sister of Charity, and was led on board blindfolded by Father Moysant, who had grown a beard. After remaining in Europe nearly a month Mrs. McDonald sailed from Europe on Sept. 25 and landed in New York. I went there to meet her, and she said she wouldn't blame me if I sued for divorce and admitted she had done wrong.

More than two hundred newspapers reported on the disappearance of Mary McDonald and Father Moysant. A German newspaper carried a heavily illustrated story accusing him of forgery. The *Chicago Herald* reported a violent confrontation between Mary and the detectives who followed her to New York. The newspaper reported that Mary threatened a detective with a knife and chased the him into the street. The *New York Times* reported that "the two conspired to poison him [McDonald] but that Mrs. McDonald was afraid to administer the poison."

From her New York hotel suite, paid for by her husband, Mary granted interviews to newspapers around the country. The *Buffalo Morning Express* reported, "She went away simply to visit the Paris Exposition and professes great astonishment and indignation at the fuss created over her leaving home and explains that the notion to make the trip entered her mind all of a sudden."

The *Galveston News* carried an interview with Mary, whom they described as educated, ladylike and forty-four years old but looking ten years younger. She said, "It is true that Father Moysant was a visitor at my husband's house. If Father Moysant disappeared at the same time that I did it is something that I can neither affirm or deny, as I know nothing about it. If it is true that he has disappeared, then it is my opinion that he has gone into some monastery in this country."

She told the *Davenport Weekly Republican* that she "cared for Father Moysant while he lay sick at her residence, but she would have done as much for any person who was ill in her home."

She demanded that the church clear the priest's name, but the Catholic Church sought to distance itself from Father Moysant. From the *Inter-Ocean*: "An endeavor is being made to show that Moysant was not recently connected with Notre Dame Church, and that he had not exercised any priestly function in that church of late....Officers of Notre Dame 'disclaimed all knowledge of him, although he is chronicled in the directory as an assistant priest there....Now apologists are being sent around to the newspaper offices.'"

She named Mike's father as the source of rumors about her and Father Moysant:

> *My father-in-law, Edward McDonald, a man 78 years old, is largely the cause of my leaving Chicago. He it was who told my husband stories about me. Often, we three have been together and grandpa has spoken evil of me and papa* [Mike] *has taken my part saying that he had the fullest confidence in me.*
>
> *In order to clear myself and Father Moysant I would have to stand on a platform and bring the church and my father-in-law face to face. It would cause a scandal in the church, but until this request is granted me I shall never return to Chicago.*

Mike remained steadfast in his belief that Mary was a victim. In a story carried by the *San Francisco Chronicle*, he explained Mary's innocence at the hands of a serial seducer: "'I am satisfied it was not a case of personal infatuation....She was weak mentally, and he was strong mentally and physically, and under his powerful leverage, the Church, he made her an easy prey.'...Twice during the interview McDonald broke into tears. Two months or so ago his little boy was sick, and he said Mrs. McDonald nursed him with the greatest devotion."

In October, the *Omaha Daily Bee* reported, "The millionaire seemed to be in a milder mood than when his wife left, and said he always knew she would return to her children. From the way he talked it looks as though the couple will soon be reunited."

But by November, McDonald sat in court with tears in his eyes as witnesses—household staff and hotel waitresses—presented proof necessary to grant a divorce. Mary, who was not present at court, did not file papers contesting the divorce, nor did she seek custody of her children.

No longer the wife of a wealthy man, Mary stayed in New York, where, ironically, she earned her living as keeper of a boardinghouse—the very thing she hated when married to Mike. Years later, Mary McDonald returned to Chicago, where once again she operated a boardinghouse.

Later in life, a close friend asked McDonald how he could be so gullible, to which he replied, "When you can't trust your wife and your priest, who can you trust?"

McDONALD BUILDS THE EL

Chicago can thank Michael Cassius McDonald for creating the Loop. Without him, downtown would lack its distinctive moniker. With the fortune McDonald earned as a gambler and his unlikely relationships with Charles Tyson Yerkes (an ex-convict from Philadelphia) and Clarence Darrow (a Chicago city attorney who in a few years would defend Mayor Harrison's crazed assassin, plead for acquittal of murderers Leopold and Loeb and champion evolution in the famous Scopes Monkey Trial), the loose ends of the El lines were joined in a loop.

Charles T. Yerkes arrived in Chicago with the intention of opening a bank, but upon seeing an opportunity to expand the city's mass transit system, he bought the North Chicago City Railway Company from the city's disgraced former police superintendent Jacob Rehm, who spent six months in prison for accepting a bribe from Michael McDonald. Yerkes added cable-driven streetcars to the system of "urban stagecoaches" in operation since the antebellum era. Jack Harpster, author of *The Railroad Tycoon Who Built Chicago: A Biography of William B. Ogden*, wrote, "When Yerkes purchased the company, he overcame the patents [owned by the City of Chicago] by employing a new technology, and his new cable railway was very successful after solving some early problems. The system remained profitable until replaced by electric cars at the dawn of the twentieth century."

In Chicago, rumors circulated that the former financial advisor to the treasurer of the City of Philadelphia, who spent time in in prison for larceny, paid bribes as a matter of course. Perhaps the rumors gained validity when the public learned that Yerkes received a pardon from the Pennsylvania governor because he threatened to release documents incriminating the governor and President Grant in shady business deals. The sale of the company to an outsider who circumvented city ordinances drew suspicion. The *Inter-Ocean* reported, "The following dispatch relative to the purchase of 2,505 shares of the stock of the North Chicago Street Railway Company throws but little additional light upon the transaction. There is a manifest disposition upon the part of Mr. Yerkes to shroud the details of the matter and the identify of his financial associates in mystery."

Yerkes told a reporter, "It is a private business transaction, in the ordinary course, without any sensational features, and I cannot disclose their names....I cannot reveal the names of the purchasers—that is a matter of private business—a large transaction, perhaps but not concerning the public."

Potter Palmer squelched Charles Yerkes's plan to build the State Street El above the State Street entrance of the Palmer House. *From* The History of Chicago *by A. T. Andreas.*

While Charles T. Yerkes built the South Side El, his much younger wife purchased jewels and dresses from Chicago's finest stores. *Library of Congress, ggbain26961/ hdl.loc.gov.loc.pnp.ggbain.26961.*

Yerkes continued his quest to dominate Chicago's mass transit with little knowledge of the city's movers and shakers, and his plan to build an elevated railway above State Street met its doom when Potter Palmer objected to noisy El trains running above the Palmer House's State Street entrance. Yerkes tried to secure a place for his wife as a member of Chicago's elite society, but Emilie Grigsby, the teenager he bedded while still married to the mother of his six children, failed to gain acceptance by Chicago's upper class. Polite society never accepted Mrs. Yerkes, but fame came her way as the model for the adulteress Aileen Butler, a character in *The Financier*, a novel written by Michael McDonald's former employee Theodore Dreiser. As William Stead wrote in *If Christ Came to Chicago: A Plea for the Union of All Who Love in the Service of All Who Suffer*, "the citizens have an incurable suspicion" of the Yerkeses.

Yerkes spent millions trying to be respectable. He bought art, as many wealthy Chicagoans did at the time. His choice: two Rodin sculptures purchased at discount before the art world came to appreciate the sculptor. He bequeathed an electric fountain to Lincoln Park, and at a cost of more than $9 million in today's dollars, he bought a telescope for the prestigious University of Chicago.

The *Inter-Ocean* questioned Yerkes's willingness to finance his projects with his own, or his company's, money and his willingness to bribe officials:

> *The question…is not whether Mr. Yerkes has a clean record, but whether he is to be given valuable privileges by the city without giving the public or the city anything in return. If the franchise asked is worth a large sum of money, why cannot Mr. Yerkes' company afford to make considerable concession to the people.*
>
> *The company, it is said, has money, and is ready to pay it out in order to get what it wants. Why should that money go into the pockets of the aldermen instead of into the treasury of the city, or be turned into benefits for the people?*

Yerkes petitioned the Chicago City Council for passage of an ordinance granting him for exclusive rights to run his cable cars through the LaSalle Tunnel. The tunnel, now an eyesore dividing lanes of traffic at LaSalle and Kinzie, was hailed as an engineering marvel when it was built in 1869 to aid the flow of traffic under the river without frequent interruption caused by raised bridges. In 1871, passage through the tunnel saved the lives of thousands who escaped the path of the Chicago Fire. The *Chicago Tribune* raged about conditions granted in the ordinance:

> *The ordinance which provides for running cable cars through the La Salle Street tunnel submitted to the City Council last night is impudent in its character. It contains one clause expressly relieving the company from liability for the repair or maintenance of the tunnel, even after it shall have been surrendered completely to the cable cars. The ordinance also carefully omits to provide for any compensation being made to the city by the company for the use of the tunnel, which cost $600,000, the annual interest charge on which is now $36,000. The ordinance ought not to be considered and cannot be passed by honest votes. We do not see how any Alderman who has the least self-respect or any regard for the interest of his constituent can vote for such a monstrous measure.*

When the ordinance came up for vote in the city council, Mike McDonald sat in the spectators' gallery coaching the aldermen, confident the council would pass the ordinance and send it to the mayor for his approval. (It was not known at that time that McDonald held a financial interest in Yerkes's company.) Later, it was reported that the aldermen who received three dollars from the city for attending the meeting received thousands of dollars from McDonald for voting in his favor.

With the deadline for the opening of the Chicago World's Fair fast approaching, Yerkes hatched an idea for an extension of his "Alley L" that ran above city-owned alleys from Congress to Thirty-Ninth Street. City fathers, who estimated that every hour 110,000 passengers would travel from downtown to the fair, welcomed the extension. Construction of the route moved quickly around factories, homes and new hotels built for fairgoers, including the mysterious lodgings owned by serial killer H.H. Holmes. When the L was completed on May 10, 1893, exhausted fairgoers who insisted on riding the "Alley L" stood in line for hours, as half-empty steamboats floated along Lake Michigan north to the city.

Finished with Chicago, Yerkes sold his stock and moved to England to develop the London Underground. He took the Rodin sculptures with him,

Passengers waited hours to board the new South Side El at the Columbian Exposition. *Library of Congress, LC-D/G-Stereo-1s08446.*

but the telescope he furnished, still the world's largest refracting telescope, is housed in Yerkes Observatory near Lake Geneva, Wisconsin—the place where astrophysicist and television personality Carl Sagan learned about "billions and billions of stars" and where astronomer Edwin Hubble, for whom the Hubble Telescope was named, worked on his postdoctorate degree. And Yerkes is forever immortalized by the Yerkes Crater, a moon crater named in his honor by the International Astronomical Union.

The Lake Street El, McDonald's pet project, connected the ends of the Loop. Though not particularly interested in mass transit beyond its financial rewards, he reasoned that a West Side El would deposit passengers near the illegal racetrack he owned near Garfield Park on Chicago's West Side.

Michael McDonald built the El line that connected the mass transit system known as the Loop. *Chicago History Museum, DN-0004591.*

Michael McDonald built the Lake Street El to transport passengers to his racetrack near Garfield Park. *From* The History of Chicago *by A.T. Andreas.*

When construction of the Lake Street El was forced to stop, McDonald asked Clarence Darrow to draft a new ordinance to allow work to continue. *Library of Congress, hec06038// hdl.loc.gov/loc.pnp/hec06038.*

McDonald didn't wish to compensate owners of frontage property on Lake Street for damage caused by battering iron supports into the street, so rather than dole out cash to property owners, he gave them soon-to-be-worthless stock. When a city ordinance halted construction of the Lake Street El, McDonald stormed city hall and ordered city attorney Clarence Darrow to draft a new ordinance: "[He] ordered that the Commissioner of Public Works issue a permit to the Lake Street Elevated Railway Company to proceed with the work of constructing the substructure of said company's railway on Lake Street in the manner in which said company has already constructed a part of said substructure, to be built hereafter, subject to the approval of the Commissioner of Public Works and the City Council."

McDonald paid thirteen aldermen bribes of between $2,500 and $5,000, or a total of $40,000, for voting in his favor. When the ordinance became law, he celebrated the victory by taking more than two hundred people on an all-expenses-paid trip to Niagara Falls.

VOTE EARLY AND OFTEN

Mike's candidate won, and the *Inter-Ocean* lamented, "Nov. 4, 1873 will go down to posterity as a black day in the annuals of Chicago. Yesterday, our rebuilt city, the pride of the United States and the wonder of the world, became the property of a bigoted, illiterate mob of Germans and Irish. Yesterday was inaugurated the reign of the worst ring that was ever organized in the West."

Throughout Michael Cassius McDonald's thirty-four-year reign over Chicago's elected officials, he employed three simple strategies: (1) unite ethnic communities; (2) handpick candidates sympathetic to their issues; and (3) win elections by any means necessary.

In 1873, McDonald joined with prominent German American Anton Caspar Hesing to defeat the Republican mayoral candidate who ran on a "law and order" platform that banned the sale of liquor on Sundays, a discriminatory law that closed neighborhood taverns frequented by immigrants who worked six days a week. In Chicago, local taverns served as more than a place to get a drink—barkeepers held mail for immigrants without fixed addresses, transcribed letters dictated by illiterate customers to their families in the old country, cashed laborers' paychecks and served hot meals to single men that reminded them of home.

Anton Caspar Hesing knew well the struggle of Chicago's German immigrants. As an orphan in Germany, the teenager followed in his late father's footsteps as an apprentice in a brewery but rebelled against his tyrannical boss and fled to America, the land of freedom. After suffering financial losses as a grocery store owner and a manufacturer of bricks, he ran for public office on the Republican ticket and won election as county sheriff, becoming the first German immigrant to hold elective office in Illinois history. The Republican ballot that year included presidential candidate Abraham Lincoln, who credited Hesing for bringing new voters to the Republican Party, writing to Hesing in part: "Our German Fellow-Citizens:—Ever true to Liberty, the Union, and the Constitution—true to Liberty, not selfishly, but upon principle—not for special classes of men, but for all men; true to the Union and the Constitution, as the best means to advance that liberty. Your obedient servant, A. LINCOLN."

As sheriff of Cook County, Hesing protected the rights of all citizens, including African Americans, as racial tensions in Chicago resulted in violent confrontations. Hesing fought off a crowd that descended on a black tradesman refused service from a teamster. Hesing intervened in an ugly incident involving an African American man named Walker who refused to leave a public, horse-drawn "bus," described by the *Chicago Tribune* as follows:

> *The driver came out from a nearby saloon and observing Walker, stepped to the window and rudely exclaimed, "Come out of here you G-d d… nigger."…In a boiling rage the driver entered the bus, seized Walker by the collar and roughly dragged him out and after getting him to the bottom of the steps dealt him a savage blow in the face. Walker had hitherto made little or no resistance, but upon receiving the blow seized the driver, threw him down, and with remarkable forbearance, did not return the blow, but contented himself with holding down his assailant, when he might have administered a summary punishment for the brutal treatment. An immense crowd rapidly gathered.*

The driver fled upon the arrival of Sheriff Hesing, who ordered soldiers from a German American regiment of the Union army to protect Mr. Walker. As word spread that Hesing was defending a black man, mobs of white males assaulted innocent African American men throughout the city. The *Chicago Tribune* lamented, "We are glad to know that Sheriff Hesing so promptly, courageously and effectually checked this instance in the bud, but the spirit [of racism] is still rampant."

When his term as sheriff ended, Anton Hesing purchased the German-language newspaper *Illinois Staats-Zeitung*, one of Chicago's largest daily newspapers, and soon found himself at odds with Joseph Medill, editor of the *Chicago Tribune*. Medill, a fellow Republican, favored the rights of native-born Americans over foreign born. Ironically, Medill was not born in the United States but was born in Canada and, as such, was a British citizen. Medill's editorials reflected his contempt for immigrants and especially for Irish immigrants:

> *There exists in this country a contemptible desire on the part of politicians to curry favor with our foreign population, in order to secure their vote.... We do not believe that American birth is a disgrace to a man, or sufficient cause to disqualify him from holding office. But the Irish Democracy of Chicago seem to think otherwise. They hold that natives are an inferior race of creatures, and not fit to take any responsible part in the government of this city—particularly in administering justice or keeping public moneys.*

Chicagoans elected Joseph Medill as mayor after the Great Chicago Fire of 1871, in part because he advocated for a stronger building code. From Medill's inaugural address:

> *Can there be any doubt as to our duty in view of these conditions and considerations? It seems to me it is obvious and imperative. Those who are entrusted with the management of public affairs should take such measures as shall render the recurrence of a like calamity morally impossible. The outside walls and the roof of every building, to be hereafter erected within the limits of Chicago, should be composed of materials as incombustible as brick, stone, iron, concrete or slate. Self-preservation is the first law of nature, so the self-preservation of the city is the highest duty of its rulers. Except for the most temporary uses, I am unalterably opposed, from this time forward, to the erection of a single wooden building within the limits of Chicago.*

Disillusioned by the treatment of immigrants in Chicago, Hesing advised German Americans to leave the Republican Party: "It is the interest and the duty of the German Republicans, who have heretofore been in the majority, to let the Democrats...step to the foreground, to give them the custody of the offices."

Hesing organized thousands of Irish and German immigrants to protest the policy that priced the poor out of the housing market and favored wealthy Chicagoans, who could afford to build their homes with costly bricks and stone. The *Cincinnati Enquirer* reported on the protest in disparaging language: "It was a noisy mob, and nothing else, being composed principally of the scum of the community—men who spend most of their time in saloons and in idleness—and half-grown boys…men who never owned a foot of ground, and never will, if they do not spend less money for beer and whisky."

Mayor Medill set about ridding the city of illegal gambling when he imposed strong criminal penalties against gambling and ordered his chief of police, Elmer Washburn, to renew raids. Yet McDonald continued to operate openly under the watch of local police officers and predicted that Medill's effort to close gambling parlors would be short-lived: "Every new broom sweeps clean, but it wears out in time." Medill's broom wore out the summer after his election, when he resigned as mayor and sailed to Europe for an extended stay.

With Medill gone, McDonald and Hesing formed an alliance to elect a new mayor. Despite pleas from German Americans to nominate Hesing for the office of mayor, he declined. Despite pleas from Irish Americans for McDonald to run, he also declined. The gambler had power to run the city; he didn't need to be its mayor. As historian Richard Henry Little wrote, "McDonald never held office, but he ruled the city with an iron hand. He named the men who were to be candidates for election, he elected them, and after they were in office they were merely his puppets."

Throughout 1873, Anton Hesing spoke in opposition to the Sunday closing law imposed by Republicans despite xenophobic diatribes in the press. In response to his work organizing Germans and Irish immigrants, the *Chicago Tribune* wrote:

> *Sly efforts were made to fuse the Germans and Irish, and it is understood that a compact has been entered into between some of the leaders of these nationalities, to the effect that the Irish shall get all, or nearly all, the offices.…Mr. Hesing is to be "Bismarck," and boss once more. He is ambitious to be again dictator, to compel men to obey his nod and beck, to order the course of events, and, though he does not desire to hold a single office, he does desire to control every office in the city and county.*
>
> *…Mr. Hesing, having talked up the tribe of which he claims to be the big chief, has invited all the other tribes to join him. But the other tribes refused to do so, and refuse to be considered as tribes.…No committee of men, however influential in past politics, can transfer the votes of the Irish citizens of Chicago to any party of which Herr Hesing is the chief, or to any alliance with Germans, or other persons of foreign birth, to opposite the portion of the people knowns as Americans.*

But the *Chicago Tribune* was wrong. The newspaper underestimated the power of Michael Cassius McDonald, who brought with him the support of Chicago's criminal underworld, the Irish American community, the National Distillers and Wholesale Liquor Distributors Association, the Saloon-Keepers League and aldermen who owned saloons (i.e., approximately 15 percent of the officials elected to the Chicago City Council).

On the eve of the election, newspapers urged citizens to vote against "the piebald rabble, headed by A.C. Hesing and lashed to the polls by the Saloon-keepers Union." And they appealed to readers to "Go to the polls! You have no business more pressing than this." The *Inter-Ocean* warned, "Mr. Colvin is a stranger to public business. It is a poor time to experiment." The *Chicago Tribune* reported that the "election of Mr. H.D. Colvin as Mayor as any time could only be regarded as a huge practical joke."

McDonald and Hesing's candidate won by a margin of ten thousand votes, many of them cast by drunken men supplied with free liquor at polling places held in Chicago's saloons. Newly naturalized citizens cast three thousand votes. Newspapers hinted at fraud. Perhaps they were correct in their assumption, but it didn't matter.

On election day 1873, McDonald set up in his gambling parlor a one-stop naturalization/voter registration/polling place where men received their newly minted citizenship papers and instructions on how to vote for Mike's candidates. If they were hungry, Mike supplied a meal and a beer. Feeling lucky? Mike gave the voters chips to redeem at the gaming tables in the back of the saloon, where games were rigged in favor of the house. Have a little extra time on voting day? Cast another ballot at Mike's place and get more chips or hitch a complimentary ride on a beer wagon to any of the other hundreds of saloons owned by members of McDonald's syndicate.

Election day in Chicago was especially violent that year. During the twelve hours the polls were open, shots were fired at voters on Chicago's West Side, in the Seventeenth Ward men were thrown into a ditch and black eyes and bloody noses were distributed throughout the city. Police refused to intervene, arresting just one man only after he attempted to disembowel another voter with a knife. The next day, Anton Hesing flew a large Prussian flag over his office building, and saloonkeepers hoisted Irish flags heralding the German/Irish victory.

In his inaugural address on December 1, 1873, Mayor Colvin reiterated his promise to abolish the Sunday closing law:

During the last municipal administration, the attention of our community has, to a great extent, been diverted from all questions referring to an economical management of the city finances, or even to the protection of life and property, by efforts as fruitless as they were frantic, to enforce certain ordinances in regard to the observation of the first day of the week. It is a well-known fact that those ordinances, how much soever they may have been in consonance with the public opinion of a comparatively small and homogeneous population at the time of their enactment, have ceased to be so, since Chicago has, by the harmonious co-operation of citizens belonging to different nationalities, grown from a village to the rank of one of the greatest cities of the world.

Mayor Colvin warned Chicago City Council members, "You may, perhaps, see fit to pass an ordinance, but remember the prerogative of the Mayor—the power to veto."

The new mayor disregarded petitions in opposition to gambling and alcohol signed by thousands of women who protested outside city hall, and within two months, the city council repealed Sunday closing laws. With that issue resolved, Colvin awaited further instructions from McDonald. Clifton Wooldridge, a Chicago detective who achieved celebrity status and dubbed himself the "World's Greatest Detective," wrote in his history of Chicago that Mike McDonald's gambling parlor was "virtually the city hall, for from his little office in 'The Store' McDonald managed the affairs of the city." Politicians mingled with gamblers day and night. McDonald need only interrupt a card game to consult with local officials.

McDonald supported the election of Irish American favorite Dan O'Hara to replace city treasurer David A. Gage, who had embezzled $500,000. At McDonald's request, the new mayor appointed Mike's friend Jacob Rehm police superintendent. Michael Cassius McDonald now owned not only the mayor's office but also the city treasury and the police department, and with the election and selection of other local officials, he moved closer toward control of Cook County.

Not all of McDonald's men were honest. Charles Kern, whom McDonald selected to run the sheriff's department, skimmed money from a fund the county allocated to feed prisoners, pocketing approximately $50 per day. City Collector George Von Hollen provided McDonald with a steady source of information and cash. Like Anton Hesing, he came to Chicago from Germany. As a twenty-year-old immigrant, he opened a grocery business catering to the tastes of Chicago's large German-born population. During the Civil War, he was captured by Morgan's Raiders, and as a civilian, he

A newspaper illustration shows the gambler's hold on local politics. *Chicago History Museum, ICHi11659.*

served with distinction as president of a popular German social organization. Backed by German Americans, he joined city politics, first as a city alderman and then as a member of the board of health and later as city collector at a salary of $4,000 annually.

As Von Hollen's influence grew, so did the gambling habit he fed with cash he pocketed from the city treasury to cover his bets at McDonald's and other gambling parlors, often losing $1,000 in a single night. In an interview with the *Chicago Tribune*, he admitted losing $10,000 at George Hankins's place, but he did not reveal his losses at McDonald's place. His debts grew and grew until he fled to Canada to avoid a lengthy prison sentence for embezzling $134,085 from Chicago taxpayers. In Canada, which at that time did not have an extradition treaty with the United States, he wrote poems and revived his career as a grocer. From time to time, the City of Chicago and Cook County dispatched lawmen to find Von Hollen. Although he had no authority to arrest Von Hollen, William Henry Heafford, the man who took over the job of city collector, took a crack at finding the fugitive. On one occasion, a deputy sheriff accompanying an insane prisoner to Detroit crossed into Canada to look for him, but neither the prisoner nor the deputy could find Von Hollen.

Curiously, George Von Hollen wrote a letter to the recorder's office in Chicago bemoaning his life up north. In the letter, published in the *New York Times*, he claimed that he was starving in Canada, had no money or friends and desired to return to Chicago. Apparently Von Hollen did have at least one friend: disgraced Chicago alderman (and gambling parlor wingman) James Hildreth, who joined Von Hollen in another business venture in Ontario. Hildreth was also a man who enjoyed the finer things in life, as evidenced by ownership of eight boats and a diamond stud, worth $41,000 today, that he claimed was "presented to the alderman by his constituents."

A year later, a Wisconsin newspaper referred to Von Hollen as a German poet: "The Governor General of Canada and the Princess Louise arrived at Hamilton, Canada, yesterday, where they had a reception. A song of welcome for the occasion was written by 'the local German poet,' George Von Hollen, formerly Treasurer of Chicago, who 'got away' with about $100,000 of the people's money."

McDonald provided Police Chief Jacob Rehm with $30,000 in exchange for access to confidential police records, and together they hatched a scheme to skim federal tax on alcohol and funnel money into the personal bank accounts of Rehm, McDonald's former political ally Anton Hesing and others. When the federal government finally caught wind of the scheme, Rehm served six months in prison and paid a $10,000 fine. Anton Hesing served three months in prison for his part in the "Whiskey Ring." McDonald sat back, unscathed.

Michael Hickey, the man who replaced Rehm as head of the police department, was no friend of McDonald. One evening, while drinking at a friend's tavern, McDonald overheard a man voice his support of Hickey; McDonald broke the man's nose and kicked him until he bled. The battered man filed a complaint with the police, but McDonald was not prosecuted.

Hickey prohibited his officers from visiting McDonald's and fired those who did. With free time on their hands, the dismissed officers spent their days at McDonald's anyway, venting their anger while knocking back free drinks. How could they support their families without a steady paycheck and bribes? Rumors swirled around these meetings, alleging Hickey's involvement in a brothel. Officers reported to newspapermen that Police Chief Hickey rented property to a brothel for a $3,500 bribe. Whether true or not, upright citizens, including Robert Todd Lincoln, the president's son, demanded his removal from office, and McDonald's friends in the city council voted to replace him with Valerius A. Seavey, who believed that legislation to outlaw gambling was useless.

As Mike's gambling business grew, so did his reputation as a thug. Unannounced raids of gambling parlors ceased because police officers "scheduled" them. One Saturday evening, McDonald went into a saloon frequented by politicians to confront owner James McGarry, who was rumored to have insulted the gambler. McDonald aimed a pistol at McGarry's head, intent on killing him, but before the gun went off, Clemmens Periolat grabbed the gun from McDonald's hand. Mr. Periolat was not a politician, however; as a supplier, he held a monopoly on Cook contracts. Periolat had a reputation for submitting bogus invoices to the county for goods supplied to the county's insane asylum, hospital and poorhouse.

Officers escorted McDonald in a private carriage to the local police station, where he boldly declared, "I own [the] Superintendent of Police." As McDonald's trial for attempted murder approached, newspapers demanded to know, "Is there power enough in the City of Chicago to put down this man McDonald? How much longer is this gambler and his gang of ruffians to be allowed liberty to carry on their nefarious operations without hinderance from the authorities? How much longer are peaceful citizens to be exposed to assault by these scoundrels, without any hopes of protection by the police authorities?"

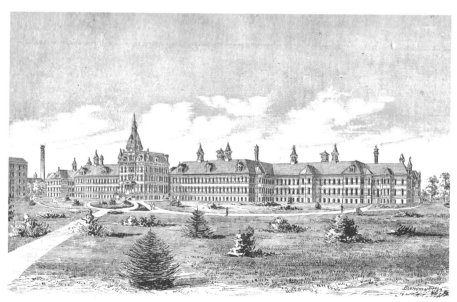

Testimony of McDonald's friend Clemmens Periolat saved the gambler from a murder conviction. Periolat was notorious for submitting inflated invoices to the county's insane asylum. *From* The History of Chicago *by A. T. Andreas.*

In December 1874, a packed courtroom watched nattily dressed, cigar-smoking Michael McDonald listen to a parade of eyewitnesses whose testimony McDonald's attorney, A.S. Trude, discredited on cross. The star witness, defendant McDonald, offered brief testimony: the gun wasn't loaded. The jury returned quickly with a verdict of not guilty. The *New York Times* reported on the verdict, adding that "McDonald is a noted gambler… the quarrel grew out of politics."

To celebrate his victory, McDonald ordered engraved invitations delivered by well-groomed messengers to Chicago's elite: prominent businessmen, politicians, clergymen, members of the board of trade and newspaper reporters. The invitations read, "The pleasure of your company is respectfully requested Saturday evening, Dec. 26, at 8 o'clock at a grand banquet to be given at the Store [Mike's gambling parlor] in honor of his triumphant vindication by a jury of his countrymen. Speeches and songs by prominent gentlemen. The Roulette wheel will play during the intermissions."

McDonald entered the Store accompanied by a police escort as cheers rang loudly, rendering introductory speeches inaudible. After dining on a sumptuous dinner, the audience listened to humorous skits in which actors portrayed McDonald's nemeses. Guests raised glass after glass of champagne toasting McDonald until the following morning as they sang, "For he's a jolly good gambler, For he's a jolly good gambler, For he's a jolly good gambler, and politician too!"

Despite Mike's efforts, Mayor Colvin did not win reelection, primarily due to circumstances over which he had no control. When the Panic of 1873 struck, the depression brought twelve thousand angry, unemployed laborers to city hall demanding food. The mayor attempted to raise money for the men by selling Lake Park (now Lincoln Park) to the railroad, but cooler heads prevailed. The following year, Chicago suffered a second major fire that destroyed more than eight hundred homes south of the Loop. The insurance industry publicly blamed Mayor Colvin for lax fire prevention ordinances and poor supervision of the fire department. Mayor Colvin's brief term in office came to an ignominious end a year later when he refused to vacate his office. From the *Encyclopedia of Chicago*:

> *In 1875 a new city charter lengthened the mayor's term from one to two years and expanded the office's powers. Because it was not clear whether the new charter extended the term of incumbent mayor Harvey Colvin, political chaos and near riots resulted when Colvin refused to give up the seat to the newly elected Thomas Hoyne in 1876. After a police cordon around City*

Hall prevented bloodshed, the court permitted Colvin to remain in office until a new election later that year.

Mayor Colvin's successor, Monroe Heath, ran on a platform of municipal reform with support from a coalition of Protestant businessmen. Under his administration, all departments reduced staff and trimmed budgets, but cutting the police department budget backfired. With police officers' salaries decreased by 25 percent and manpower reduced, citizens complained that "the average policeman is seldom, if ever, upon his beat…a fight or robbery, occurring in broad daylight is almost invariably an old occurrence before a policeman can be found, or voluntarily puts in an appearance."

But during Mayor Heath's term of office, raids on McDonald's place ceased after his old friend Judge McAllister rebuked the police department for ordering the unlawful invasion of McDonald's premises: "Officers in uniform may constitute a mob, and their tumult amount to a riot just the same as an unlawful assemblage of men in rags and filth…they were violent and tumultuous…the police power of the city of Chicago, where the individual personal rights of the citizen are habitually disregarded to my certain knowledge."

McDonald chose as successor to Mayor Heath Carter Henry Harrison Sr., a disgraced congressman who fled Washington under of suspicion of authorizing fraudulent payments to bogus Civil War veterans. The Yale graduate whose familial lineage included an uncle who signed the Declaration of Independence, cousin Bill (William Henry Harrison, the ninth president of the United States) and cousin Ben (Benjamin Harrison, the twenty-third president of the United States) had little in common with Mike McDonald, the barely educated son of illiterate Irish immigrants.

After seven years in Congress, Carter Harrison retreated to his mansion in Chicago, where he threw himself a lavish welcome home party attended by three hundred well-to-do Chicagoans. The *Inter-Ocean* described the evening of March 6, 1879, this way: "The grounds were brilliantly lighted by means of two bonfires and the parlors were all ablaze with the illumination in honor of the event. The house is one of the finest on the West Side and showed off to the best advantage under the artistic arrangement it had undergone in view of the return of its proprietor. The chief order of the hour was mutual congratulation and social chat."

Lauded at his gathering among his friends, his popularity didn't extend to thousands of working Chicagoans, who considered the Kentucky-born gentleman a southern sympathizer. The *Chicago Tribune* warned that the

Michael McDonald handpicked Carter Harrison, who served five terms as mayor of Chicago. *Library of Congress, LC-USZ62-134211.*

election of Harrison would notify the world "that the people of Chicago welcome the Southern Brigadiers as conquerors and rulers." Harrison was McDonald's choice and public opinion didn't matter.

Harrison played coy and did not immediately seek office, insisting that he came to Chicago as a private citizen and had retired from politics, but at the urging of McDonald, the de facto head of Chicago's Democratic Party, he accepted the nomination and campaigned energetically throughout German American and Irish American communities. He assured citizens that they could gamble and, if they so desired, drink on Sundays. Harrison maintained that these were the God-given rights of all Americans. On election day, McDonald's henchmen rounded up voters from houses of ill repute, saloons and gutters and even registered seventy-five underage voters, all living at the same address. Again the press cried fraud, but with McDonald's support, Carter Harrison Sr. was elected to four consecutive terms as mayor.

Carter Harrison showed his gratitude toward McDonald almost immediately, appearing at McDonald's gambling parlor on a regular basis, and when keno's popularity threatened McDonald's roulette wheels and card games, Harrison strengthened ordinances.

McDonald defended Harrison's administration in his own way. After John Gelder of the Second Ward left a meeting where he had delivered a speech criticizing the Democratic machine, Mike followed him outside and then hit and kicked him to the sidewalk. Although the incident attracted a large crowd, McDonald was not arrested.

Publicly, Mayor Harrison denounced Mike's friend Jimmy Carroll, but privately he did nothing. It was a well-known secret that McDonald played host to the notorious bank robber James Carroll of the Carroll Gang, often allowing him to spend the night in a spare room above the gambling parlor. Mayor Harrison, who was well aware of Carroll's location, vowed to reporters, "So help me [god], I'll break up Carroll's gang…if I have to break up every house in the city." But he did not order the police force to arrest Carroll. A plainclothes detective finally arrested Jimmy in the company of

McDonald and an assistant state's attorney, who protested that the arrest was illegal. Jimmy was taken to a courthouse downstate by McDonald's attorney, A.S. Trude, to face an eight-year prison sentence, but he managed to escape to Canada, where he robbed banks until the Canadian authorities sent him to a prison in Kingston, Ontario. Mike McDonald convinced Mayor Harrison and several judges and aldermen to sign a petition for the release of Jimmy Carroll, but the mayor later denied to the press his involvement, claiming that McDonald had hoodwinked him into signing a document he had not read.

When police arrested a McDonald associate for fencing stolen property, Mike whispered to the mayor that the police superintendent might like to retire and suggested Captain William McGarigle as a replacement. McGarigle allowed McDonald to operate his gambling parlor without police interference and went about the business of upgrading the police department with a new system of call boxes that allowed citizens to report crimes. Buoyed by praise from policemen everywhere for introducing innovative technology to the police department, the superintendent embarked on a three-month tour of Europe, ostensibly to acquaint himself with police methods used in London, Paris and Vienna.

When McGarigle's term as police superintendent ended, he continued a life of public service. With McDonald's support, he rose through the ranks of the county political machine to become warden of the county hospital, but his life of public service ended in 1887 when McGarigle was convicted on corruption charges. Among the charges were that he had a private horse stable built on the hospital grounds. He purchased expensive damask drapery for his office and spent large sums of taxpayer money on liquor, claiming that the money was used to purchase surgical dressings for the hospital. One evening, while sitting in jail awaiting sentencing, he asked Sheriff Matson to drive him to his family home on Racine Avenue. No problem. The sheriff took him home and waited as McGarigle greeted his wife and children but became suspicious when the prisoner did not return from a trip to the bathroom. Advised by a child that her father was taking a bath, he waited an appropriate amount of time and then broke down the bathroom door. By then, McGarigle was on his way to Canada. Months later, a bottle was found in the waters of Lake Michigan near the town of Grand Haven, Michigan. A note inside read, "To my friends in Chicago: A few more hours and I will be safe through the straits and in Canada. Sheriff Matson, please accept my thanks for the bath, but I have concluded it in British waters. Oh Ed [Mike McDonald's brother], I wish you were here with me! Goodbye till we meet!"

When prosecutors cited McDonald's name in a nationwide investment scam, he needed someone with more power than Mayor Harrison to smooth things over with the federal government. Although McDonald is credited with coining the phrase "Never give a sucker an even break" long before W.C. Fields uttered these words, he was only tangentially involved in a type of investment scam that would become known as a Ponzi scheme. McDonald's friend and McGarigle's cohort Frank Loring ran the investment swindle from an office on LaSalle Street, where he netted $1 million from suckers around the world. McDonald was not indicted, but he provided attorneys to represent Loring, who received a small $500 fine and one year in prison. But that was not the end of the matter. New York

McDonald handpicked William McGarigle to head the police department. McGarigle later fled to Canada to avoid a prison sentence following his conviction on charges of corruption. *From* The History of Chicago *by A.T. Andreas.*

gangsters demanded a pardon for their pal Frank Loring and appealed to Mike for help. Mike traveled to the White House, where he chatted with President Chester Arthur for a few minutes and left with his signature on a document that set Mr. Loring free.

Carter Harrison served three full terms as mayor in a temporary office building, but thanks in part to Michael McDonald, he spent his fourth term in a brand-new building. The Great Chicago Fire of 1871 destroyed the massive Italianate structure, built in 1853 for the City of Chicago and Cook County to conduct official business. The fire destroyed thousands of vital records, the bell that alerted citizens to the catastrophic fire and the rotunda where President Lincoln's body lay in state in May 1865.

When the fire's glowing embers died, the government opened temporary offices in a busy West Loop police station and then hastily constructed a building around an iron water tank that housed the nascent Chicago Public Library; pigeons that nested inside gave the building its name, "the Rookery."

Local government offices remained among the books and the birds for more than a decade, long enough for Michael Cassius McDonald to infiltrate every level of local government and cozy up to captains of industry and

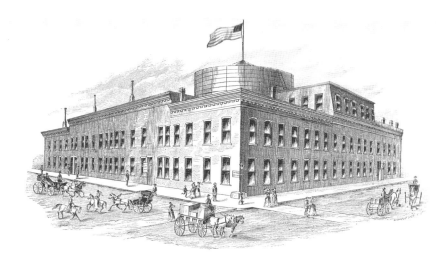

After it was destroyed by the Chicago fire, city hall temporarily relocated to a structure surrounding a water. Officials stayed in the temporary building for more than ten years until McDonald built a new city hall. *From* The History of Chicago *by A. T. Andreas.*

influential businessmen. Because of these relationships, local government awarded him a contract to provide stone for the new building. Unlike the Irish immigrants who quarried the stone, McDonald simply sold it—at inflated prices.

Irish immigrants, clutching axes and shovels from sunrise to sunset from 1836 to 1848, whacked away ninety-six miles of solid rock to construct a canal that would link Chicago's port on Lake Michigan to the Gulf of Mexico via the Mississippi River. The idea was first proposed in the seventeenth century by explorers Father Marquette and Louis Joliet, who observed the difficulties Native Americans and French fur traders faced portaging their heavily laden canoes across marshy land between the lake and the river. The project brought prosperity to Chicago and displaced St. Louis as the rising star of the Midwest. When the canal opened, cargo too heavy to transport on freight trains could easily sail the length of the United States from its border with Canada to the Gulf of Mexico. As the backbreaking work continued through two Illinois towns, Joliet (named for the explorer) and Lemont (originally named Athens), the Irish noticed a difference in the type of stone they chiseled. In these two villages southwest of Chicago, their shovels hit limestone, a hard rock formed millions of years ago from shells and skeletons of marine animals.

McDonald determined to use the limestone discovered by Irish immigrants instead of a harder, more durable stone like granite. The fix was in, but for the sake of appearances, McDonald formed a bogus company and chartered "a private train stocked with venison and wines to ferry the commissioner out to the Lemont stone quarries" to verify the quality of the stone.

But by the time new building was complete, it was already obsolete. According to author Wendy Bright of *Chicago Architecture*, "Problems beset this building from the start and talk of replacing it started almost as soon as it opened…the interior was problematic: tall ceilings with small windows and dark, drafty corridors.…Plus, the building had taken so long to complete that it quickly proved inadequate."

Worst of all, the limestone Michael McDonald had supplied began to break, and chunks of heavy stone plummeted to the street below, narrowly missing pedestrians who walked past the building. No problem, McDonald would fix it, but again he needed to make it appear that a legitimate company had the solution. He called on Henry Holland, a longtime associate and as yet unindicted gambler, to work with the self-proclaimed Professor Lundberg, who held a proprietary formula guaranteed to treat decaying stonework. Working together, their company, the American Stone and Brick Preserving Company, gained the endorsement of the *Inland Architecture and News Record*:

> The American Stone and Brick Preserving Co. seems to be growing in popular favor in the protection of building walls in this city, as is evidenced by many of the prominent buildings treated by their process…
>
> The company is now at work applying their preserving compounds to the decaying stone work of the Cook county hospital and has secured the contract to treat and preserve our crumbling court house. The Lundberg process, as used by this company, is indorsed by prominent business and scientific men, and its durability established by the test of time.
>
> The American Stone and Brock Preserving Co. will guarantee that building walls treated by their process will remain in a sound state of preservation for at least ten years and claim as follows: …building walls can be water-proofed and preserved without the least changing their natural color…building walls can be restored, water-proofed and preserved, with or without materially changing the original color of the stone or brick, or colored to suit the owner.

The *Inter-Ocean* also supported the miracle product:

One of the most perplexing questions of the age, and one which scientific men are largely interested in, is the preservation of stone and brick in buildings from the ravages of several and changeable climate. A process meeting this demand has recently been invited by Professor C.O. Lundberg.

We deem it our duty, independent of side issues of whatever kind, to express our present opinions in an impartial way, based upon such facts, which thus far, we have been able to gather.

Professor Lundberg, too, has not only improved upon his old process, but has invented, as he asserts, a new and better one, which he feels assured will fill all the necessary requirements for the preservation of building stone and brick, and will also serve the purpose of arresting the progress of disintegration and scaling of old building walls of whatever kind.

In addition, it should be borne in mind that his process is highly thought of and recommended by a number of prominent citizens, as well as scientific men, the opinions of whom are worthy of consideration.

It will be but a short time before this company will have no superior in rank and magnitude and will fully meet one of the greatest wants of the age.

In 1886, the American Stone and Brick Preserving Company was awarded a contract to preserve the crumbling building. For months, laborers applied the Lundberg fluid to the courthouse. Citizens hoped for a miracle, but didn't get one. It turned out that the formula was nothing more than linseed oil and lead paint, which did nothing to preserve the stone.

When the project was completed, both size and costs had been inflated. The building, which measured 240,000 square feet prior to application of the proprietary formula, swelled to 440,000 square feet upon completion. Holland's original estimate of $30,000 was revised, and Holland submitted an invoice for more than $180,000 to include McDonald's cut plus bribes the gambler paid to government officials.

In less than ten years, the building was in such a poor state that it was demolished. McDonald was not involved in its replacement: the granite and terra-cotta structure that still stands in downtown Chicago.

After serving four terms as mayor of Chicago, Carter H. Harrison Sr. called it quits, his reputation tarnished by his handling of the 1886 demonstration for an eight-hour workday by laborers that resulted in the death of police officers and protesters when a bomb was thrown into the crowd at the Haymarket Square near what is now the entrance to the Kennedy Expressway.

Right: Michael McDonald spent $30,000 to elect Dewitt Clinton Creiger as Chicago's twenty-sixth mayor after Creiger promised to reopen gambling parlors. *From* The History of Chicago *by A.T. Andreas.*

Below: During Carter Harrison's term of office as mayor, a peaceful demonstration for the right to work an eight-hour day ended in the death of seven police officers. *Library of Congress, ppmsca1956//hdl.loc.pnp/pp.print.*

"THE FIRST DYNAMITE BOMB THROWN IN AMERICA" MAY 4TH 1886.

THE PERSONNEL OF THE GREAT ANARCHIST TRIAL AT CHICAGO.
BEGUN MONDAY JUNE. 21 ST 1886 . ENDED FRIDAY, AUGUST, 20 TH 1886.

McDonald spent $30,000 to defeat the reelection of John A. Roche, who succeeded Harrison. McDonald replaced Roche with Dewitt Clinton Creiger, who reopened gambling parlors shut by the previous administration. According to *The Chicago Sports Reader: 100 Years of Sports in the Windy City*, "Creiger was apparently opposed to the reopening of the gambling houses which had on their walls the accumulated cobwebs of two years while Mr. Roche was mayor. Friends came to his rescue and induced him to promise that the gambler should be permitted to resume business at their old stands....Mr. McDonald exercised the talents which have made him famous and wealthy."

Harrison traveled the world, bought a newspaper and stepped away from politics, but by 1892, he felt an itch that needed a good scratching, or as Erik Larson wrote in his book *Devil in the White City: Murder, Magic, and Madness at the Fair that Changed America*, "By the end of 1892, however, he had made it clear that he would love to be the 'Fair Mayor' and lead the city through its most glorious time but insisted that only a clear signal of popular demand could make him actually enter the campaign."

But Carter Harrison had had a falling out with McDonald, now himself the owner of a newspaper, the *Chicago Globe* (which employed the not-yet-famous novelist Theodore Dreiser), and the pair railed against each other in their respective newspapers. A few months before the mayoral election, McDonald was asked to comment on Harrison's severe criticism of the gambler in Harrison's *Times* newspaper. McDonald quipped, "I never read the Times, and I was not even sure that it was in existence. If the paper sees fit to roast me, why it will only add to my popularity. What Carter Harrison says has no weight whatever with the Democratic party."

A reporter from the *Inter-Ocean* asked Michael McDonald if he would be Chicago's next mayor, to which he replied, "I won't say that I am a candidate, but who knows what may happen? Candidates are springing up every day and strange things happen in politics sometimes. I have often been asked if I didn't want this or that office, such as some assessorship or collectorship, or some other kind of ship. What do you suppose a man like me wants with such offices? Why, I wouldn't take any of 'em if there were fetched to me on a silver platter. No, sir: not a one of them. Your uncle Michael Cassius is not ambitious in that line."

Michael McDonald had moved on to state politics, campaigning for his friend John Peter Altgeld, who owed a debt of gratitude to the gambler who had procured a judgeship for Altgeld years earlier, and with McDonald's influence, Altgeld was elected Illinois's first Democratic governor since

Michael McDonald assured Mayor Harrison that pickpockets would not enter the Columbian Exposition. *Library of Congress, LC-USZ62-104795.*

the 1850s. He didn't need to support Harrison, but the two gentlemen set aside their differences for the sake of the World's Fair of 1893. McDonald agreed to keep gamblers and pickpockets away from the fair's entrance, and if caught, each offender would pay a ten-dollar fee to the arresting officer and leave the area immediately. The amount of money collected by the police, the gamblers and the politicians during the World's Fair can only be imagined. In his extemporaneous exposé of Chicago, *If Christ Came to Chicago*, English investigative journalist William T. Stead wrote, "A colossal fortune was divided. Many people had a finger in the pie before the residue reached Harrison."

In return, Harrison promised visitors a safe but wide-open city under his fifth term as mayor of Chicago. According to author Emmett Dedmon, Harrison "purchased a supply of two hundred barrels of whiskey for official entertaining," and factories worked overtime churning out roulette wheels to satisfy the city's sudden demand.

Credit for bringing the World's Fair to Chicago, constructing the famous White City and attracting enough visitors to the fair to turn a profit rests with farsighted Chicagoans who sought to show the world that Chicago was not just "the wickedest city in the world." Among them were department store owner Marshall Field, meatpackers Philip Armour and Gustavus Swift and inventor of his eponymous reaper Cyrus McCormick, each of whom raised millions in financing; chief architect Daniel Burnham, who designed the buildings; and local art teacher and sculptor Lorado Taft, who sculpted classical adornments for the buildings and then hired a team of women he referred to as his "white rabbits" to install the embellishments.

During the six-month-long World's Fair, Chicago welcomed more 27 million visitors, including serial killer H.H. Holmes and two of his victims, and introduced the world to Wrigley's Juicy Fruit gum, Pabst Blue Ribbon beer, Aunt Jemima pancake mix, the Ferris wheel, Cracker Jack, zippers and fax machines. Mayor Carter H. Harrison personally greeted prominent visitors, including President Grover Cleveland, Nikola Tesla, Scott Joplin, Helen Keller, Frederick Douglass and Princess Eulalia of Spain.

A few days before the fair ended, Mayor Harrison left the fairgrounds early, complaining that he was "dead tired." A carriage brought him to his mansion on the city's West Side, and perhaps anticipating a long evening with Annie Howard, his thirty-year-old fianceé from Mississippi, the sixty-eight-year-old mayor took a nap on the couch. At approximately 8:00 p.m. that evening, Mary Hansen, the family maid, answered the door for a visitor who introduced himself as Mr. Prendergast, a city official who had come to the mayor's house to discuss his appointment as Chicago city counsel. According to Chicago historian Ray Johnson, "Mayor Harrison was known as the mayor whose door was open to anyone and that would ultimately be his undoing." Mary was unaware that the delusional man felt that although he worked distributing newspaper and did not have a law degree, he was owed the position in exchange for voting for Harrison in the last election. The maid told the man to wait in the vestibule, but Eugene Patrick Prendergast didn't wait for her to return. Seething with anger, he searched the house for the mayor. When he found the mayor, he shot him three times, and twenty-seven minutes later, Mayor Harrison was dead. His last word was "Annie."

Clarence Darrow, Michael McDonald's old friend from the city council, defended the mentally ill Prendergast, hoping to save him from the hangman's noose, but Eugene Patrick Prendergast was executed on July 13, 1894.

McDONALD, HIS SECOND WIFE
AND HER TEENAGE LOVER

Michael Cassius McDonald was known as a gambler, a political fixer and a thug, but to the children who lived on Ashland Avenue, he was a nice man who gave the kids a pat on the head and a piece of candy. Among the boys and girls who flocked around the generous millionaire was his future wife, Flora.

Rabbi Fogel Feldman and his wife, Frances, were not particularly friendly with the Michael and Mary McDonald. The Prussian immigrants did not attend lavish balls at the McDonald house or attend church with the family, but their children played together. The Feldman boys caused their parents no trouble, but their daughter Flora was stubborn, belligerent and unstable. From a young age, she insisted everyone call her Dora, not Flora. She craved attention, and despite her religious father's objection, she embarked on a short-lived career as an actress, preforming under the stage name "Madam Alberta." When that didn't work out as she had imagined it would, she stalked Sam Barkley. Sam, a professional baseball player who is remembered primarily for a contract dispute involving his status as a free agent. Mr. Barkley resisted her advances, but the eighteen-year-old showed up out of the blue in his Kansas City hotel room and threatened to kill herself if he didn't marry her. Despite his initial feeling that Flora, now Dora, was crazy, he married her, and she gave birth to their son, Harold, whose presence put a damper on the couple's glamourous lifestyle.

When Sam's injured knee ended his career as a professional baseball who earned $3,000 a month, the couple couldn't afford to pay their bills, so they moved to Pittsburgh, where Sam had connections from his days playing for the Pittsburgh Alleghenys. Sam's friends helped him buy a cigar store, but with little experience as a business owner, the shop was not a success. With few resources, the couple moved to Chicago, where they sought refuge in the Feldman household. Dora reignited her career as an actress, and Sam scraped up enough money to open a sleazy saloon in the red-light district.

At a benefit for the Chicago Fire Department, McDonald noticed the girl from Ashland Avenue dancing on the stage. Little Flora was now a grown woman named Dora. Despite her parents' objection, he began escorting the beautiful young woman around town, well aware that she was a married woman with a small child. Just like the baseball player, he thought her unstable. McDonald wanted to marry Flora Dora Feldman Barkley and even agreed to adopt little Harold Barkley, but her husband needed to be convinced to

Michael McDonald paid pro baseball player Sam Barkley $30,000 to divorce the woman who became McDonald's second wife. *Library of Congress, bbc.0071f//hdl.loc.gov.loc.pnp/bbc.0071f.*

divorce his unfaithful wife. Mike's "friends" followed Sam Barkley around town to persuade him to give up Dora, and when the court granted a decree in the case of *Barkley v. Barkley*, Sam was $30,000 richer.

Michael Cassius McDonald, age fifty-nine, and Flora Dora Feldman Barkley, age twenty-six, were married in a Catholic church in Milwaukee, and they kept news of the marriage private until the Chicago newspapers noticed the couple sitting in the audience of a performance of *The Bauble Shop* at Hooley's Theatre. A reporter who inquired about the young woman's surname described her only as a smiling woman in a sealskin coat. McDonald would not reveal any information about her, simply stating, "It is enough to say M.C. McDonald is a married man....It is my own affair. The public is not interested." But in a few years, the public would be very interested in the new Mrs. McDonald.

The first few years of their marriage were happy. The old man seemed to have gained a new vigor, showing off his young wife at Chicago's finest restaurants, attending fancy dress balls in support of Jewish and Catholic charities and inviting the elite to private concerts at the McDonald mansion on Ashland Avenue. But all was not well in this blended family. Mike's sons Cassius and Guy, who had been abandoned by their mother, Mike's first wife, Mary Noonan Goudy McDonald, hated the idea that their former playmate was now their stepmother and a little stranger named Harold was their brother. To escape the drama that occurred on an almost daily basis in the McDonald household, nineteen-year-old Guy married his girlfriend despite his father's vow to disinherit him. The feud reached its apex when Dora took her stepson to court for writing scandalously improper letters to her at the Ashland Avenue address. The court cleared him of all charges when he revealed the author of the letters—his mother—but the family dynamics grew more complicated as Dora realized the power Mike's ex-wife held over his sons.

Perhaps because of Mary's reappearance, Mike decided to move the family from the fifteen-room mansion on Ashland Avenue to an even larger home, an eighteen-room mansion on tony Drexel Boulevard, just a few doors down from John Shedd, president of Marshall Field & Company and a philanthropist who would later donate his fortune to the eponymous Shedd Aquarium. Of course, Dora loved the idea of living among Chicago's elite, and she abandoned her ties to Ashland Avenue and kept in touch with only one person from the neighborhood, Webster Guerin, her teenage lover.

The affair began when the boy was just thirteen years old. One morning, while Dora glanced out her parlor window, she noticed a ginger child and his brother walking down the street to the local elementary school. Just a glimpse at Webster Guerin and she was hooked. With the same energy that ran through her body as the teenager who stalked a baseball player, she pursued the boy. She invited him in after school, stroked his beautiful red hair and pinned a photo of herself to his school clothes. Soon the boy was spending more time at the McDonald household than at his home. If Mike found it strange that his wife filled her afternoons entertaining a thirteen-year-old, he kept his suspicions to himself. Perhaps he noticed or perhaps Dora and the boy concluded their lovemaking before Mike returned home. But the dangerous intimacy was not unnoticed by the boy's mother and aunt, who confronted Dora. Years later, the *Chicago Tribune* interviewed the aunt:

"We went to see Mrs. McDonald about Webster," said Miss Fitzgibbons [Webster's Aunt Nellie] simply. "We never had been friends, and it was hard, but his mother determined to do something." Mrs. Guerin asked Mrs. McDonald: "Why are you going around with Web all the time? He would be a good boy if you would only let him alone. You have your husband and I have only my boys. Won't you leave them to me."

Mrs. McDonald laughed. "I am not going around with Web," she said. "I heard that Guy [her stepson] told Dad [her husband] that. When Web comes back from California I am going to have him kill Guy."

"Then my sister got down on her knees to that woman." She cried and said: "Please let that boy alone. He would be good if it was not for your influence. You seem to have cast a spell over him. I can't do anything with him anymore. O, won't you let me have him?"

"I am not running around with him" she repeated.

"Didn't I catch you at Richard Vaughan's house [a reference to Dora's brother-in-law] with him the other night?" asked my sister. "I saw you running out of a room with your hair all flying, I know what you are doing."

Then I said to Mrs. McDonald: "Aren't you ashamed and you a married woman, too?" She put her hand back of her dress as though to get a weapon.

"I'll kill you," she said. "Look out; look out!"

She was still crying this when we left the house. After this we could not do any more with Web.

The affair continued for ten years as McDonald grew old, no longer interested in dining out or spending an evening at the theater; he no longer enjoyed a physical relationship with the woman who now called him "Papa."

Dora continued to shower her young lover with trips and expensive gifts, including a diamond tie stud. After a decade, Webster no longer found Dora attractive, but he needed her money to finance a photography studio that was simply an excuse for the young bachelor to charm women into buying photographs placed into inferior, overpriced picture frames.

One morning in February 1907, after Dora's maid finished dressing her in one of many stylish outfits, Dora came down to breakfast distraught. Trembling, she confessed to her husband that she was being blackmailed but that she was determined to put an end of it.

McDonald later told a reporter from the *Chicago Record-Herald*, "My wife appeared very nervous and her actions were unusual. She said 'I am tired of being blackmailed and I am going to stop it. Today I will settle it.' While the language was strange I did not take it seriously and laughed. 'Let me attend to it if anyone is trying to blackmail you. Put the matter in my hands. I know how to deal with such things, for I have been blackmailed myself in my life.'" But Dora didn't wait until evening to settle the matter. Soon after the conversation with her husband, she headed straight for Webster Guerin's studio. By noon, he was dead.

Newspapers around the world jumped on the sensational story of a young man and his older lover, the wife of a wealthy gambler. Despite the lack of eyewitnesses to the shooting, the press reported the event in great detail with some degree of accuracy. From the *Cincinnati Enquirer*: "The tragedy of Salome, brought down 2,000 years, was re-enacted in Chicago to-day when a jealous woman, young and beautiful, acting as executioner, shot the man she loved, and then, as he lay dying, wiped the blood from his lips that she might have his last kiss....As a result of the tragedy Chicago is to have a trial that will surpass in interest the famous Thaw case." (This last mention was a reference to the murder by New York millionaire playboy Henry Thaw of famous architect Stanford White, who was rumored to be the lover of Thaw's teenage wife, Evelyn Nesbit.)

From the *Salt Lake Herald-Republican*: "One of the most sensational murders in the history of Chicago was committed today when Mrs. Dora McDonald, wife of millionaire Michael McDonald, the former gambling king, killed Webster S. Guerin, a well-to-do portrait artist. [She] threatened death before she fired....In her hand was a smoking revolver....In the room Guerin lay dead. He must have expired instantly."

From the *San Francisco Examiner*: "The police have gathered evidence which they declare will prove the killing a carefully planned assassination by a desperate and revengeful woman. In prison the woman raved wildly at intervals during the day, her actions studied by a group of six noted alienists [mental health experts]....The name of Webster Guerin or the details of the tragedy formed no part of her ravings."

The *Inter-Ocean* speculated on a motive: "The woman's relatives say the tragedy was provoked because Guerin blackmailed her. Friends of Guerin insist that he was the victim of a woman scorned."

The *Wilkes-Barre Times* put forth the theory that Mary had an accomplice: "When Guerin was shot he fell under a sink, but when the police arrived the body lay six feet in the middle of the floor, showing conclusively that it had been moved after death. Mrs. McDonald was physically unable to do this owing to Guerin's weight, and the police argue that a man aided her."

There were no witnesses to the shooting, but there was no doubt that a gun was fired and Webster Guerin was dead. The two people who were with Dora when she arrived at Web's studio—his brother, Archie, and an office boy, both of whom had met Dora on several occasions—recounted events that happened prior to the shooting. Archie said that Web told him and the office boy to leave for a few hours. Dora and Webster were left alone in the studio, and the door was closed. A gunshot was heard throughout the building. Three tenants working below Guerin's studio—Lorenzi Blasi, Charles William and Jacob O'Neill—recalled that they raced upstairs to Guerin's office, where they found Dora, her face

Webster Guerin began an affair with Mrs. Dora McDonald when he was a teenager. *Chicago History Museum, DN-0004681.*

and hands bleeding, attempting to crawl through the locked door as she smashed the glass pane with a pearl-handled gun. They pulled her through the shards, and Mr. Blasi took the gun from her as she screamed, "He shot himself. Get a doctor quick. For God's sake, get a doctor or he will die."

Coincidentally, five minutes later, Clifton Wooldridge, Chicago police officer and self-proclaimed "World's Greatest Detective," happened to arrive at the Guerin brothers' studio to investigate reports of their shady business practices. The detective immediately took charge of the crime scene.

Near the body, Wooldridge found a handwritten poem that read, "Kill me, if you will, for all is well, I know that to Satan your soul you can't sell. I have saved you from everlasting hell; I lifted you up, when low I found, slowly but surely you were dragging me down."

The police brought the hysterical Dora McDonald to the Harrison police station, where she wailed, "If he is going to die I'll say that I killed him, and then they will kill me, too. I don't want to live without him." A police matron administered a sedative, and when Mike arrived a few hours later, the drugged woman appeared calm. She embraced her husband and said, "You know you would be better off if I were dead. Put your arms around me, papa. I want you near me. I told you I would have to go away; that was the cause of all the trouble. I told you that I had to go away; I wish you

The pearl-handled gun that Webster gave Dora McDonald for Christmas was found at the murder scene. *Chicago History Museum, DN-0004683.*

would let me. You stay, dear papa. For the rest I do not care. I am all right so long as you are here. I want to go home, papa, I want to go to my beautiful pink room with the canary bird. I don't like it here. They are mean to me."

Suddenly, she became frantic and raved so loudly that prisoners in other cells demanded that the police matron remove Dora. As the staff made arrangements to transfer her to the women's annex, she yelled to McDonald, "He pushed me in a chair, papa and I won't let anyone talk to me like that. I am glad you came, papa, and everything will be all right now. You wouldn't listen to me and I wouldn't listen to you and something happened."

She flung herself on the floor and had to be carried to the annex, where her rambling continued. She babbled that a darkened room was filled with crying children. "I want you to give a party for those poor babies. Can't you hear them crying? She claimed that the sun's rays had burst through her head and that a storm swept through a ship as she sailed across the ocean. Throughout the night, McDonald held her hand, stroked her hair and cried softly so that she wouldn't hear him.

McDonald left the jail to make arrangements for her release. As he walked from the building, he spoke briefly to a reporter from the *Inter-Ocean*, one of many members of the press waiting for juicy details firsthand: "Mrs. McDonald has not been well for some time. She has been hysterical for more than a week and has been under the care of her mother."

McDonald's attorney, A.S. Trude, accompanied him on his next visit to the jail. McDonald refused to allow court-appointed physicians to examine her. "Get out of here, both of you," he shouted as he pushed the two doctors away from Dora's bedside and threatened to physically throw them out if they did not permit his wife to rest. The family's lawyer, A.S. Trude, expressed his outrage to the press: "It is the worst outrage I have heard of in thirty-five years of practice. A prisoner in the jail is immune from such invasion, and the courts have held so time and again. I am going to see if the physicians who violated this rule cannot be prosecuted."

When Dora's condition worsened to the point that the staff feared for her life, McDonald allowed Dora's maid, Trude, and Dora's uncle Ben, also an attorney, to observe doctors as they examined her. Police surgeon Dr. J. Ettelston and family physician Dr. Leonard St. John listened as the warden postulated that the cuts on her hands and face resulted in blood poisoning, and a concerned nurse reported that Dora's pupils were dilated, though probably as a side effect of opiates administered hourly. The doctors completed their examination and concluded that if the semi-comatose woman did not receive nourishment soon, she would be dead by morning.

The family doctor told the *Inter-Ocean*:

> *Mrs. McDonald should be taken away from here as soon as possible. The surroundings here are not of a nature to aid her in the recovery of her senses and I think that she should be taken to some place like the Garfield Park Sanitarium, where she will be given every opportunity to recover. I cannot say whether or not she will ever regain her sanity. She is at present passing through the crisis in the course of her hysteria which may pass off and leave her perfectly sane or may render her incurably insane. The shock to her nervous system must have been a most severe one, especially as she had not fully recovered from an attack of hysterics which kept her in bed for nearly a week.*

The police surgeon offered his optimistic opinion of Mrs. McDonald's condition: "I think that early next week we will have restored her to a rational mental condition. She has had a severe shock, without a doubt, but I hardly think that it will result in permanent insanity."

Even the inspector eagerly waiting to take Mrs. McDonald's statement chimed in with his amateur diagnosis: "I do not think Mrs. McDonald is insane. At least that is my judgment of her mental condition based on considerable experience in cases of this kind. She is laboring under a great stress and probably is as nervous as any woman would be under similar circumstances. I think that by tomorrow she will be in a condition that will admit my putting a few questions to her. So far, I have not been able to hold any conversation with her. She is wrought up and rambles greatly, but she is not insane."

The State of Illinois hired its own team of mental health professionals who witnessed her alternate between silent, glassy-eyed stares and hysterical laughter as a police officer served her with an arrest warrant. But Webster Guerin's aunt, Nellie Fitzgibbons, wasn't buying the claim of temporary or irreparable insanity: "She is an actress. She has always been clever that way, and I believe that she is now acting a part and is absolutely in her right mind. Now that she has killed Webster she is probably unwilling to accept the consequences of her actions. I have no faith in her pretended insanity."

While the rest of the Guerin family grieved, brother Archie attended to the business of identifying his brother's body at the McNally & Duffy Funeral Home. The sight of Webster laid out on a slab brought him to tears, but when he felt a comforting arm around his shoulder, he stopped sobbing and was shocked to see that the comforting arm belonged to the husband of the woman who murdered his brother. "Boy. I want to talk with you and sympathize with you. Come with me. The worst for you is over, but I have mine still to face." The two men spoke privately for ten minutes before McDonald hurried off to visit Dora in jail. What they spoke about in private is unknown.

As Archie collected his brother's personal effects, he noticed that the diamond stud Webster always wore was missing. Archie knew that Webster wore the stud on his tie the day he was killed; he saw it when the police removed the body from the crime scene, but the undertaker insisted that a cheap glass stud was on tie when the body arrived at the funeral home, not the birthday present from Dora worth $250. Was it stolen at the chaotic scene in the photography studio, or did it find its way into the hands of someone at the funeral home? The detective who worked the crime scene

Archie Guerin identified the body of his brother, Webster. *Chicago History Museum, DN-0052253.*

adamantly refused to believe that his men would steal from the body of a murder victim: "I am certain the stone could not have been changed before the body was taken from the studio. Nobody who chanced to enter the place at that moment would have had time to substitute the paste affair. Patrol Driver Gable, who carried the body to the undertaking rooms, has been a driver for more than twenty years and has the confidence not only of his superior officers at the station, but of Chief of Police Collins."

Suspicion turned to the man who handled the body at the funeral parlor: Jesse Thames, a well-known, and supposedly reformed, career criminal. The police investigated but did not charge Jesse with the theft, and the diamond was never recovered.

One week after the scene at the funeral parlor, McDonald and his son Guy attended the coroner's inquest, at which Archie testified:

Mrs. McDonald came into the office about ten minutes after 10 o'clock, while Web and myself were discussing this affair.

I had been remonstrating with him about the woman. "Web," I said, "why don't you leave town and get rid of her." He had seemed much concerned about the affair of late and seemed depressed about it. "Well," he said, "will you go with me?" I said I would. Then he said, "The business just now is so that I can't leave it, but I will go away with you in May."

Shortly after that Mrs. McDonald came in. She appeared nervous and excited. "Well, I'm done with it now," she said, "I told that old slob I'm all through with him. I'm going to New York tomorrow."

Upon hearing his wife's unkind words about him repeated in open court, McDonald's "jaws closed with a jerk and his eyes fairly bulged out with a defiant look" as he leaned on his son Guy. Archie Guerin continued:

Web told her not to get so excited and didn't appear to be particularly concerned about her going away.

"But don't imagine that I am going away and leave you before I put a bullet in your head."

At that she told me to leave the room. I didn't make a move and she started at me as if to strike me. Web stepped between us, and said to me: "All right, Arch, you go and let me take care of her. I can calm her."

Before that he had asked the office boy, Hansen, to leave the room because he didn't want him to witness any scene. I left and didn't come back until a little after 12 o'clock and saw the body of my brother lying on the floor.

When asked if Dora had ever threatened to kill Webster, Archie recalled the evening Dora waited outside the Powers Theater, where he and his fiancée, Avis Dargan, had seen a show. Despite Archie's suggestion that they talk the next morning, she followed the couple to a restaurant and sat at their table, where she shouted to Archie, "Don't you think he ought to be killed for throwing me over the way he has?"

Archie's testimony turned to the pearl-handled revolver found at the murder scene: "Last Christmas she gave him a pair of gloves for a present, and he asked me what he had better give her. 'She wants a pearl handled revolver.' He said. I told him he was foolish to give her anything like that, but he had a way of doing his own will, regardless of advice of others. She once created a scene in a hotel by flourishing the revolver in the presence of Webster and her brother. I don't know whether she intended shooting herself or someone else at the time."

One of the men who found Dora and the pearl-handled gun testified next: "She cried, 'He shot himself; he shot himself; save him' as she smashed through the glass. After hearing the shot, I opened the door, about two seconds before Mrs. McDonald broke through the glass. She had no revolver in her hands, but I saw one lying on the floor beside Guerin, and she went and picked it up."

Detective Dougherty, who accompanied Wooldridge to Guerin's photography studio to investigate his shady business practices, testified:

> "O, God, tell me if he is dead," she said, tearing her hair when I entered. "Don't blame me! You have a mother—I picked up something shiny and threw it out the door. He shot himself. He thrust me back in a chair and struck me."
>
> "What is your name?" I asked.
>
> "I don't know, no matter; can't tell you. Ask him."

Detective Clifton Wooldridge, who did not witness the shooting, nevertheless recited his version of the events. When he finished his testimony, Coroner Hoffman commended Wooldridge for the thoroughness of his search of the crime scene and chided the other police officers for not gathering more evidence.

More than twenty-five witnesses testified throughout the day. At 8:00 p.m., the coroner's jury rendered a verdict that sparked rumors that McDonald's men had bribed members of the jury. As to the cause of death, the verdict was inconclusive: "Webster S. Guerin came to his death from shock and hemorrhage due to a bullet wound in the chest, and from the evidence presented, we the jury, are unable to determine whether the said bullet wound was fired from a revolver held in his own hand or otherwise."

With the coroner's inquest closed, and with no possibility of reconvening, the state's attorney conferred with the coroner in a closed-door session before announcing his intention to submit the case to the grand jury. At the insistence of Dora's attorney, A.S. Trude, Judge Newcomer allowed a preliminary hearing to be held in the jail's hospital so that Dora would not have to suffer the strain of appearing in a courtroom.

With Mike at his wife's bedside, she remained motionless. The room was quiet as a nurse stroked Dora's hair, but when a witness mentioned Guerin's name, she whispered, "Why is it, O God, tell me what it means?" Suddenly, Webster's Aunt Nellie leaned over Dora and screamed, "Murderess, you killed Web!" Dora raised her head from the pillow but could not respond coherently; she simply babbled. Dora was not questioned by the state or the defense, and at the end of the hearing (described in the press as "one of the shortest ever held by a Cook county grand jury"), Dora was indicted for the murder of Web Guerin and released on $50,000 bond.

At midnight, Dora left the county jail under her own volition via the rear door, and the following morning, newspapers speculated about her whereabouts. Would McDonald welcome her back to the family's eighteen-room mansion on the city's South Side? Did Dora leave Chicago?

The husband who had stood by her side for five weeks and paid her $50,000 bail sadly told the *Inter-Ocean* the following day, "All I know is that she is to be taken to her mother's house. Her mother and brothers are making all the arrangements. Of course, I will pay the expenses. I don't know whether I will call on her there or not. I don't know who started the idea that she was coming back to my house. It is funny that someone always knows my business better than I do."

While Dora convalesced in the bosom of her family, Mike's health deteriorated. Newspapers reported on Mike's appearance and worried that the formerly robust gambling king had become a "pathetic figure of the old man...[he] aroused more pity than any other person connected with the case."

While Chicago waited months for the trial to begin, reporters tried to keep the McDonald name in print whenever the most inconsequential events occurred. Reports included the false statement that McDonald returned to the Roman Catholic faith he abandoned when he met Dora (he never left the church) and that she resumed attendance at the local synagogue in their old neighborhood on Chicago's West Side (possibly true, as she had not converted to Catholicism as had been reported). In an obituary of nurse Mary Keegan, who cared for Dora while she was in jail, the newspaper concluded, "Pneumonia contracted when Mrs. Michael McDonald was being held at the Harrison street jail annex was likely the cause of the nurse's death." Son Guy was sued for an unpaid hotel bill of $220, and Mike received a summons to pay $90 to a music professor who helped Dora write a song about her love for Webster Guerin. Mike's

Michael McDonald (*right*), seen here speaking with an unidentified man, was an old man when he married Dora. *Chicago History Museum, DN-005145.*

sons told the *Inter-Ocean* newspaper that their father planned to begin divorce proceedings. In an attempt to avoid further connection with the McDonalds, Archie Guerin and Avis Dargan kept the date and place of their summer wedding secret. Dribs and drabs of news continued until McDonald's death on August 8, 1907.

Newspapers across the country reported his death. From the *Buffalo Courier*: "Michael Cassius McDonald is dead. Like a tired child going to sleep, the man who had once held the political destinies of Chicago in the hollow of his hand, who had been king of the gamblers and despotic ruler of the underworld that bowed in homage, passed to his final [reward] in the hospital of St. Anthony de Padua today."

From the *Pensacola News Journal*: "After only a brief illness, Mike McDonald, head of the Chicago gambling fraternity, died last night in the hospital of St. Anthony de Padua. In the certificate of death 'heart failure' is set down as the cause, but in reality, his end was hastened, if not actually brought

Mike McDonald (*left*), believing his wife's innocence, paid for her attorneys but died before the murder trial commenced. *Chicago History Museum, ICHi-21714.*

about, by the arrest of his second wife, Mrs. Dora McDonald, for the alleged murder of Walter [*sic*] S. Guerin, a young artist."

Finally, in January 1908, Judge Theodore Brentano, the former assistant city attorney who had for years raided McDonald's gambling parlor and sanctioned the destruction of his gambling equipment, began jury selection. The *Appleton Post* speculated that the prosecutor would not seek the death penalty due to "the unhappy life of the woman and her present mental and physical state." Nevertheless, Assistant State's Attorney Edward S. Day questioned potential jurors on their ability to impose the death penalty on Dora: "Under the law one of the penalties provided for murder is death. Does this meet with your approval, the defendant in the case being a woman? Can you not conceive of a case where you would vote the death penalty, the defendant being a woman?"

Potential juror Charles McGrath was not questioned about his views on the death penalty but volunteered, "I think it is only fair to say that I am unalterably opposed to the death penalty, your honor. I was not asked concerning this point in my examination, but I wish to explain my position."

Dora's attorney, Mr. James Hamilton Lewis, questioned members of the jury pool on whether their religious views would cloud their thinking: "Would it prejudice your opinions to find that the defendant was a Jew of Catholic affiliations?"

Both the defense and prosecution decided that no Jews would sit on the jury; at least five Jews were disqualified on the first day. Mr. Lewis explained his decision: "We don't want a Jew on the jury because it would place him in an embarrassing position. And I suppose it is for the same reason that the state holds the same idea. I fear that a Jew might lean backward on his conviction rather than be placed in the light of having favored one of his race."

Throughout the day, attorneys examined jurors, while Dora appeared listless and uninterested. But when Dora suddenly collapsed, Lewis stopped his examination. He called for a recess and hurried the jurors out of the courtroom while Dora's nurse led her into a side room, where she was examined by a doctor, who pronounced her weak and exhausted. It was not the testimony of the jurors that unnerved her but remarks from spectators, mostly women, whose comments on Dora's clothing, her demeanor and her sanity were overheard. "They are calling me a murderess. I can hear them saying it and I can't stand it any longer. Don't make me go back there."

Was she faking? Or was Dora really weak and exhausted? The state's attorney, Rittenhouse, addressed her histrionics with this question to potential jurors: "If during the trial the defendant, a woman, should faint or create a scene of some kind, would that in any way arouse your sympathies for her so that you could not give the state a fair and impartial trial?"

While the court was in recess, Archie spat to reporters, "She can make a fortune on the stage. She is a great actress, that is all there is to it. Insane? No more than I am, but I couldn't make believe as well as she does."

By the time Dora returned to the courtroom, even Judge Brentano had grown weary of the proceedings: "I will hold court Saturday, both morning and afternoon sessions, in order to complete this jury before Monday. We have spent five days already and have made little or no progress during the past two days. I expect this jury to be completed before we adjourn Saturday, and I hope the attorneys will assist me as much as possible."

Jury selection continued through Saturday. Fourteen men were disqualified for their apparent failure to convict on circumstantial evidence, but by Saturday afternoon, satisfied with selection of the

Dora Feldman Barkley McDonald stood trial for the murder of her young lover. *Chicago History Museum, DN-0052222.*

final juror, Judge Brentano cautioned the men not to discuss the case among themselves and granted them permission to attend the theater on Saturday evening. As the judge wrapped up the proceedings, Dora became wildly excited, beckoned to her attorney and pointed at the jury box: "What is that woman doing there? I don't want a woman to try me. She won't give me a fair trial." Mr. Lewis looked in the jury box, where only men sat. (The State of Illinois did not allow women to serve on juries until 1939.) "That is all right, Mrs. McDonald. Don't get excited. There isn't a woman on the jury." She retorted, "Yes, yes, yes there is. Can't you see her? Can't you see her?"

Mr. Lewis managed to convince his client that no woman would serve on the jury. Dora stared straight ahead as she walked through the crowd of spectators—the largest in the history of Chicago—as they craned their necks to get a good look at the murderess.

That evening, Dora retired to the Sherman House Hotel, where her late husband had provided rooms for her, for her nurse and, on another floor, for her defense team. As James Lewis, P.H. O'Donnell, Ben Schaffner and Frank Cain weighed variations of their defense strategy—self-defense, insanity or the victim's own suicide—Dora burst into the conference room, only partially clothed in a bathrobe, shouting, "My boy Harold is asleep in this room and he needs more bed coverings." Mr. Lewis replied, "Your son is at school in Deland, Florida." He motioned to Dora's nurse, Mrs. Beck, who tried to restrain her as she yelled to the group her dissatisfaction with her attorney's manners: "The newspapers are always publishing stories about how polite Lewis is. I think he is rude. He does nothing but ask me impertinent questions about my husband. I told him I had no husband—that my husband ran away and left me many years ago."

When the public read about her outburst, some speculated that she was perfectly sane and attempting to delay the start of the trial. Whether Mr. Lewis believed his client to be insane or if he simply grew tired of her behavior, he announced that Mrs. McDonald would appear in court on Monday even if he had to carry her in on a cot.

The following morning, attorney J. Hamilton Lewis delivered his opening statement:

First, I want to clear your minds, gentlemen, from any apprehension that it is the purpose of the defense to plead insanity as an excuse. The defense admits no shooting on the part of the defendant which calls for an explanation of insanity. The defense will establish that this shooting was done in self-defense, not by her hand but by the hand of the deceased while she was struggling to turn from her body the deadly hand which was leveled there.

This will be established by circumstantial evidence. So far as insanity will be brought to your attention we will show merely such a state of mind and body that you can readily see justification for her actions. The tragedy has left a shock from which she never will recover. It has left her a blank to all that has happened subsequent to the shooting.

Lewis leaned in to address the jurors stroking his odd, but completely natural, pink whiskers, as he portrayed his client as a frail young woman, unable to recover from the birth of her son, Harold, years ago. Left alone by the child's father, a professional baseball player named Sam Barkley, she fell under the spell of a powerful man, Mike McDonald:

Out on the west side, where she lived, the Guerins were near neighbors. The families were intimate. The Guerin boys were constant companions of her stepsons, Guy and Cassius, and constantly were running in and out of the house. Webster, particularly, edged himself into her household as a friend of Cassius. She felt an affection for him as a mother might have felt. Guerin went into the haberdashery business after a few years and her friendship continued to the extent that she patronized his store two or three times to help him, but that was all.

He continued reciting his well-rehearsed story of Dora's innocent desire to help the boy, the child who played with her stepsons:

Thus, Webster Guerin grew to manhood. Far from lacking in strength, far from being the weak boy that a woman could abduct, he displayed all the evidences of maturity and knowledge of the world. There was no experience with women he did not know. There was not a resort [brothel] on the west side where he was not known. As the needs of his business grew Guerin appealed to his friends, the McDonalds, for money. In one instance he borrowed $700 to raise a mortgage on the Guerin home.

Now we begin to see the career of this weak, innocent young man in all its cruel light. He had to have money. The world was his feeding ground. There was no place where the red lights glow that did not appeal to him as evening came on. His pleasures were of a peculiar kind. He had to have money, I say.

Lewis paused for dramatic effect before revealing his theory that Guerin planned to blackmail Dora. He told the jurors that Guerin and his business partner had stolen Mrs. McDonald's monogrammed stationery, composed salacious love letters to which they forged her signature and demanded $10,000. When Dora caught wind of the scheme, she was not angry, she did not solicit her husband's support and she did not end their friendship. Ever the kind, forgiving mother figure, she offered to take him to dinner at a luxurious restaurant. As they dined, Dora told Webster that she wanted him to confess his sins before God. "Come to a church and swear it. Not until then can I trust you again." Lewis continued, "Setting aside the scruples of her ancient faith," the pair walked to Holy Name Cathedral, where she led him down the somber nave to the altar and demanded that he confess his "crimes against this woman and her family." But that did not put an end to his need for money. Guerin asked Dora for money to move to New York. She gave him $250—an amount equal to $6,600 today—but he only got as far as Cleveland before he ran out of money and returned to Chicago to ask for more.

Mr. Lewis told the jury that following the incident, Dora made a half-hearted attempt to commit suicide with a bottle of chloroform. At her husband's suggestion, Dora took a much-needed vacation in California with her niece, Ethel Martin, to avoid Guerin, but "like a serpent the young man cunningly made his way to Los Angeles and confronted her."

At trial, Ethel testified about the confrontation with Guerin. "When Web began to swear at Mrs. McDonald I told him that he ought to be ashamed of himself, and that I would tell Uncle Mike and he would blow his head off, to which Web replied: 'If you say anything I guess I can do some blowing off myself, and don't you forget it.'" Dora asked her niece to leave the room and return later in a few hours. By the time she returned, Web was gone. Later, Ethel discovered photographs of her aunt in various stages of undress. Dora told her niece that Web had taken the photos for fun. Together, the two women departed for Chicago, and on the trip home, Dora attempted to commit suicide by flinging herself from her first-class compartment on a speeding train but was saved by her niece and a Pullman porter.

Lewis continued with his tale of poor, innocent Dora after her return to Chicago. "He bled her for more money, whispering of slander day and night. She gave him the money she should have used for the house. She stripped her rings from her fingers. She crept like a driven beast at his feet."

Lewis called two women who had never met Dora but could confirm that Webster had threatened her. Millie Lagen, a shopkeeper from Wisconsin, recounted an evening she spent in a Chicago restaurant a few months before the shooting. While enjoying a modest supper, Miss Lagen heard an argument at the next table between a couple whom she identified to police as Dora McDonald and Webster Guerin.

Millie heard the woman say, "I can't give you money, you know I can't get it." Then the man said, "I must have it. I will make trouble for you if you don't get it for me. You know I am in debt. You must get it for me, Dora!… Get it from the old man. You know he has more than he deserves."

Next, Mary Campbell testified about a conversation she overheard one evening as she returned to the dry cleaner where she worked. According to Mrs. Campbell, Dora wept as Web yelled at her, "I must have money. You must get it for me." To that Dora replied that she couldn't get the money, but she resolved to tell her husband, who would forgive her. "You are, are you? I will kill you now. I will murder you!" He grabbed Dora by the throat with both hands and began to strangle her. Mrs. Campbell shouted, "Don't hurt her!" and Webster fled. Both women stuck to their stories under cross-examination by the state's attorneys.

As the trial continued, Dora's attorney became irritable and inexplicably lashed out at Webster's brother. At one point, Lewis turned around to the spectators' gallery to gauge their reaction to his remarks and saw Webster's brother, Archie. Something about Archie incensed Lewis. During a recess earlier in the trial, he had accused Archie of speaking with a potential jury and physically shoved him aside. Once again, Archie got under his skin.

"Ah, my little, insignificant friend," he shouted, shaking his finger close to Guerin's face. "You can sit there with your little sniveling laughter, but—." An attorney for the State of Illinois rose to object.

"You will please confine your remarks to the subject in hand, Colonel Lewis," said Judge Brentano.

Lewis complained the next day that Webster's sister-in-law winked at the jurors and made comments such as "O, listen to those lies." To placate Lewis, Judge Brentano asked the woman to find a seat in the rear of the courtroom.

Dr. M.L. Harris was called to the stand to offer his testimony as an expert witness. Without emotion, he pinned on the wall a chart showing a cross-section of the human torso and began an anatomy lesson. "Imagine that a man has been sawed in two just below the shoulder and you are looking down into the body," he explained, pointing out the various organs, the aortas, the esophagus, the heart, the trachea and so on. Next, he examined People's Exhibit No. 3, the victim's bloody coat. "Blood from the bullet pierced the aorta, rushed into and filled the severed trachea, or windpipe, shut off the breath, and gushed from the mouth. Webster Guerin was drowned by his own blood."

Dora leaped from her chair and shrieked, "Come back to me, come back to me. I love you yet!" before collapsing into the arms of her nurse, who motioned for an attorney. After a brief consultation, the weary attorney carried Dora from the courtroom. When it became obvious that Dora would not return, Judge Brentano adjourned for the day.

Rumors of witness tampering and payoffs by McDonald's men spread throughout the press. Police detective Wooldridge testified about a promise he made to Mike McDonald to "get the little girl off any way you can." For his involvement with McDonald, Wooldridge received a three-week suspension and was forced to surrender his badge. Under examination by the court, Herman Hanson, the office boy Webster ordered out of the studio on the day of the shooting, admitted that he received a five-dollar per diem from the defense, equivalent of his weekly salary. Hanson also said that the state's attorney, Mr. Rittenhouse, threatened to arrest him if he did not change his testimony. Rittenhouse bristled at the accusation and warned that witnesses who committed perjury would suffer the consequences of their actions.

The question of whether Dora would take the stand was answered when her attorney issued a statement that due to her mental condition she would not take the stand in her own defense: "There really is no necessity of Mrs. McDonald going on the stand. Of course, we feel that for her to relate the story of the shooting practically would acquit her without further effort, but that is out of the question. Mrs. McDonald while showing signs of improvement physically today, is as much an enigma mentally as ever. She appears to take no particular interest in her case."

Two weeks of testimony came to a sudden end when Mrs. McDonald's attorneys announced that their case was closed. Her attorneys decided not to introduce evidence of Dora's mental health. It was a simple case of self-defense: "in a moment of supreme strength, with death in front of her, she seized the weapon he had taken from his desk and pointed at her and forced it back toward his own body." By dismissing medical health expert witnesses who had examined Dora, the attorneys closed the door to rebuttal by the state and the introduction of evidence incriminating Dora. Attorney O'Donnell advised the court that "Mrs. McDonald's sanity is not a question in this case and the testimony of the experts would not be admissible." Following this statement, Judge Brentano called for a conference in his chambers to sooth the angry prosecutors and allowed the state to introduce a love letter written by McDonald that would show that Dora's failed attempt to regain Guerin's affection resulted in her shooting him.

A furious Mr. Lewis asked why the letter was not read earlier in the trial. The prosecutor explained that the letter "disappeared," only to resurface in a handwriting expert's office after the trial began. Dora had written, "My Dear Web: Do you know the more I think the more I realize you are the darn[d]est chump I ever saw....You are like a foolish sportsman who leaves the favorite for the field. The field wasn't much to start with and was pitted against a favorite that was a REAL favorite with YOU....I'll wage you had put all you had on the favorite, for the field proved that they wasn't worth the powder to blow them up, and the favorite was and is in fine condition."

After weeks of testimony, Mr. Lewis gave an impassioned closing argument that brought spectators to tears:

Punishment? Can any punishment surpass that which already has fallen upon this homeless, hopeless, helpless woman? The doors of tomorrow are shut upon her. The hand of friendship has been withdrawn. The faces she loved have been averted. Where in death or imprisonment can there be such punishment as will be hers with the world turned against her and her child—the blood of her heart—scorned as the son of a woman who has been tried for murder?

Which one of us would care to have a sister or a woman dear to us go to the life she will face ever after freedom? Her days are darkness.

Veering into the obscure, ancient text that Lewis relished, he told a tale of God and angels on Judgement Day, though probably incomprehensible to his audience with the exception of a few familiar words. Nonetheless, he continued:

The great Persian Sadil tells of a man and woman who started out together. The days of the man were lighted by sunshine, his nights by stars. He reached the end of his journey at the gates of God and demanded his reward like a victor. Not so the woman. She listened to the allurements of hope and the whisperings of love. She wandered through devious ways where her hands were torn, and her feet were bruised, and her heart was made to bleed. She, too, reached the gates at last, not on her feet, but on her knees, as one whose only cry was, "Lord, be merciful."

And the great master called Amalfi, the angel of judgment, to judge her. The angel took the woman away. When they returned her face was radiant. The master demanded of Amalfi: "How have you judged her?" He answered, "As one who was miserable, a woman in agony, whose days have been sadness and whose night all misery."

And the master said: "Stand up, come forth and be free. For it is for such as thou that God gave his strength to men that they might take woman by the hand and lead her to where she may hear the Christ say: 'Come unto me all ye that labor and are heavy laden and I will give you rest.'"

And the hosannahs of the angels rang out their approval as God proclaimed, "With what judgment ye judge, it shall be judged to you again."

His story completed, he paused and addressed the jury directly, appealing to their obligations as husbands and fathers:

Gentlemen, I do not know what decision you will make in this case. But I trust whatever it is it will console your future steps by day and comfort your pillow by night. And if when you return home some woman near to you shall ask "How did you judge her, as one who was miserable, a woman?" Or, if there be a little one who noted your absence and shall come close and say, "Tell me about it, did you send back to her little boy his mamma?"

I rest my case on the fact and the law. I scorn to ask twelve sensible men to violate the law. I demand that you execute the law. For Mrs. McDonald I ask justice. I ask it on the law and the facts.

State's Attorney Rittenhouse presented a closing argument laced with jabs at the opposition, referring to Mr. Lewis as a "shyster" and "pettifogger" and the leader of a dirty defense team that committed perjury, bribery, treachery and the buying of witnesses. He accused Inspector Wheeler and Detective Wooldridge of misconduct on behalf of their friend Michael Cassius McDonald, who he claimed asked the men to bottle up evidence. He addressed the self-defense theory:

Remember insanity is altogether out of this case. The defense does not claim Mrs. McDonald was insane either at the time of the killing, before, or after it.

[Guerin] could not have inflicted upon himself the wound that killed him.... The gun never was in the hands of Webster Guerin that day. It was in the hands of Dora McDonald and she killed her sweetheart because he was tired of her and wished to break away from her and marry some chaste girl.

Mrs. McDonald began to feign insanity before the body of her victim was cold. From that moment the state has had not only to contend with lying, pretense, perjury and bribery, but with treachery, official hostility, and lack of duty.

This case is watched in every city in the country, and the mothers of 10,000 other boys are looking to you to say that such crimes shall not be tolerated in this city. If you are satisfied beyond a reasonable doubt, treat this woman as if she were a man. And in the future, when some woman shoots a man on the street you need not say, "This would not have happened if I had done my duty." I ask for justice; for a verdict which satisfies your conscience. If you believe Dora McDonald shot this man down, give us a verdict that will protect other men. Don't let sentimental women believe they can kill men in cold blood. Give us a verdict according to your conscience.

It took the jury only five hours to render its verdict: not guilty.

Dora wasted no time recovering from her fragile state of mind to thank the jury members as they collected their belongings from the jury box. Each of the twelve jurors shook Dora's outstretched hand as she told them in a whisper, "I knew God was with me, if no one else was but I thank you, all the same." With their service no longer needed, the twelve men returned to obscurity.

That evening, Dora held an impromptu press conference in her hotel suite. Dressed in a pink dressing gown, flanked by her attorney and her nurse, she stroked a bouquet of red roses in her lap as she responded to a reporter's question about the verdict: "Am I glad that I am acquitted. Well, do you know I haven't given it much thought. I prayed and prayed not to hear any of the bad things that were said....I want to go away where it is bright. I want to see the green grass and the flowers again. I'm tired of all these cars and this black, noisy city. But I don't know where to go."

A reporter suggested that she visit her son, Harold, at school in Florida. She considered his words as though she suddenly remembered she had a son: "I never had thought of that. That is a good suggestion. I think I shall do that; yes, I will." Sensing that Dora was tired, or that she might say something she would regret, her nurse escorted her out of the room.

But the world had not heard the last of Flora Dora Feldman Barkley McDonald. A few weeks after the trial, she began work on an autobiographical play, but it was never produced. She ran off to Mexico with an executor of her husband's estate, Benjamin Goodrich, a married man whose wife objected to the relationship. She battled with McDonald's first wife over which of the two was his one true legal wife. Dora sued her stepson Guy over thousands of dollars of missing jewelry. She married again, becoming Flora Dora Feldman Barkley McDonald Newcomb. Upon her death in Los Angeles on July 1, 1930, she donated $12,500 to Jewish charities in California and Chicago.

CONCLUSION

Michael Cassius McDonald never held public office, but he engineered elections, giving rise to Chicago's tongue-in-cheek practice to vote early and vote often. He didn't fight in the Civil War, but he convinced hundreds to join the Union army. Although poorly educated, he ran a major metropolitan newspaper. He wasn't an eloquent speaker, but he added to the American vernacular: "Never give a sucker an even break," later attributed to film star W.C. Fields; and "There's a sucker born every minute," often credited to showman P.T. Barnum. He never wrote a book, but novelist Edna Ferber immortalized him in *Showboat* as flashy riverboat gambler Gaylord Ravenal. He won big and he lost big playing cards, but he retired as a gambler to create "The Store," a luxurious gambling parlor the likes of which was never seen again. He pistol-whipped his opponents but doled out candy to kids on the block. As a millionaire, he moved to a mansion in Chicago's poshest neighborhood, but polite society shunned him. Michael Cassius McDonald was uniquely a Chicagoan.

BIBLIOGRAPHY

Other Materials

Bright, Wendy. "A History of Chicago's City Hall and Cook County Building." Chicago Architecture, January 26, 2015. https://www.chicagoarchitecture.org/2015/01/26/a-history-of-the-cook-countycity-hall-building.

Mayor Harvey Doolittle Colvin Inaugural Address, December 1, 1873.

Mayor Joseph Medill Inaugural Address, December 4, 1871.

The Metropolitan Museum. Costume Department. Evening dress, no. 1983.6.

Periodicals

Brick. "Revival of the Suit." Vol. 1, 1894.

Chicago Legal News: A Journal of Legal Intelligence. "Assault and Battery—Justification—Right to Defend One's House." Vol. 11, 1879.

Inland Architect and News Record. "Stone and Brick Preservation." Vol. 7, February 1886.

Official Proceedings of the Board of Commissioners of Cook County, Illinois. "In the Matter of the Contract of H.L. Holland." 1886.

Paint, Oil and Drug Review. "Trade Notes." January 16, 1889.

Books

Blevins, Win. *Dictionary of the West.* Seattle, WA: Sasquatch Books, 1993.

Currey, J. Seymour. *Chicago: Its History and Its Builders: A Century of Marvelous Growth.* Vol. 2. Chicago: S.J. Clarke Publishing Company, 1918.

Dedmon, Emmitt. *Fabulous Chicago.* New York: Random House, 1953.

Deyrup, Marta, and Maura Grace Harrington. *The Irish-American Experience in New Jersey and Metropolitan New York: Cultural Identity, Hybridity, and Commemoration.* Lanham, MD: Lexington Books, 2014.

Dubinsky, Karen. *The Second Greatest Disappointment: Honeymooning and Tourism at Niagara Falls.* New Brunswick, NJ: Rutgers University Press, 1999.

Gardner, William. *The Life of Stephen A. Douglas.* Boston: Roxburgh Press, 1905.

Gould, Benjamin Apthorp. *Investigations in the Military and Anthropological Statistics of American Soldier.* Cambridge, MA: Riverside Press, 1869.

Grossman, James R., et al. *Encyclopedia of Chicago.* Chicago: University of Chicago Press, 2004.

Harpster, Jack. *The Railroad Tycoon Who Built Chicago: A Biography of William B. Ogden.* Carbondale: Southern Illinois University Press, 2009.

Hennepin, Louis. *Nouvelle Découverte d'un Très Grand Pays Situé Dans l'Amérique.* Utrecht, Netherlands: Guillaume Broedelet, 1697.

Karamanski, Theodore J., and Eileen M. McMahon. *Civil War Chicago: Eyewitness to History.* Athens: Ohio University Press, 2014.

Larson, Erik. *The Devil in the White City: Murder, Magic, and Madness at the Fair that Changed America.* New York: Crown Publishers, 2003.

Leyendecker, Liston E. *Palace Car Prince: A Biography of George Mortimer Pullman.* Boulder: University Press of Colorado, 1992.

Lincoln, Abraham. *The Collected Works of Abraham Lincoln.* New Brunswick, NJ: Rutgers University Press, 1953.

Lindberg, Richard C. *The Gambler King of Clark Street: Michael C. McDonald and the Rise of Chicago's Democratic Machine.* Carbondale: Southern Illinois University Press, 2009.

Nash, Jay Robert. *Hustlers and Con Men: An Anecdotal History of the Confidence Man and His Games.* Lanham, MD: Rowman & Littlefield, 1976.

———. *People to See: Anecdotal History of Chicago's Makers and Breakers.* Piscataway, NJ: New Century Publishers, 1981.

Reading, Amy. *The Mark Inside: A Perfect Swindle, a Cunning Revenge, and a Small History of the Big Con.* New York: Random House, 2012.

Riess, Steven A. *The Chicago Sports Reader: 100 Years of Sports in the Windy City.* Urbana: University of Illinois Press, 2009.

Sauerwein, Stan. *Soapy Smith: Skagway's Scourge of the Klondike.* Alberta: Altitude Publishing Canada, 2005.

Stead, William T. *If Christ Came to Chicago: A Plea for the Union of All Who Love, in the Service of All Who Suffer.* Chicago: Laird & Lee, 1894.

Taylor, Troy. *Murder and Mayhem in Chicago's Vice Districts.* Charleston, SC: The History Press, 1999.

Valone, Thomas. *Harnessing the Wheelwork of Nature: Tesla's Science of Energy.* Kempton, IL: Adventures Unlimited Press, 2002.

Wentworth, John. *Congressional Reminiscences.* Chicago: Fergus Printing Company, 1882.

Newspapers

Appleton Press. "Telegraph News." January 9, 1908.

Austin American-Statesmen. October 3, 1886.

Baltimore Sun. "Great Fires in Chicago." October 9, 1871.

Belfast News-Letter. "The Destructive Fire in Chicago." October 12, 1871.

Buffalo Courier. "Ravings of Murderess Declared to Be Sham." February 23, 1907.

————. "Wife in Cell[,] Husband Dies." August 10, 1907.

Buffalo Morning Express. "Amusements." February 11, 1870.

————. "Mike M'Donald's [*sic*] Wife Returns." October 9, 1889.

Buffalo Times. "Her Husband Not a Saint." October 11, 1889.

Chicago Record Herald. January 31, 1908.

Chicago Tribune. "Buckminster's Restaurant." August 11, 1870.

————. "Burial of 'Mike' McDonald Serves to Open New Chapter in His Troubles." August 13, 1907.

————. "Camp Equipage." November 18, 1861.

————. "Carter After Mike: He Didn't Know the Times Was Still in Existence." March 9, 1892.

————. "Chicago Under Martial Law. No More Running Away." August 9, 1863.

————. "Citizens of Chicago." November 4, 1873.

————. "The City Election." November 5, 1873.

————. "Cotton Packing and Sorghum Refining in Chicago." January 29, 1863.

————. "The Dens in the Sands Broken Up." April 21, 1857.

————. "Fire Limits. How the Better Class of North Siders Feel on the Subject." January 21, 1872.

————. "The First Blood. Mike M'Donald [*sic*] Pounds an Anti-Machine Man Who Dared to Criticize His Course." June 27, 1884.

————. "Grand Congratulatory Banquet at the Store." December 27, 1874.

————. "The Great Fire. Continuation of the Investigation by the Board of Police." November 25, 1871.

————. "The Great Rebuilding." October 9, 1872.

————. "Gunnies! Gunnies!" February 27, 1861.

————. "Helpless on Hospital Cot, Alleged Slayer of Artist Is Bound to Grand Jury." March 17, 1907.

————. "Horses Wanted." September 24, 1863.

————. "How Gamblers Are Going through Mike McDonald's Pile." August 20, 1873.

————. "Judge McAllister Discharges Mrs. McDonald and Gives a Series of Slaps to the Police Force." December 3, 1878.

————. June 8, 1886.

————. "A King Who Had Us in His Back Pocket." October 2, 1988.

————. March 29, 1879.

————. "Mike a Married Man. Chicago's Noted Ex-Gambler Takes Another Wife." January 16, 1895.

————. "Mother on Knees to Mrs. M'Donald [*sic*]." January 28, 1908.

————. "Mr. A.C. Hesing Sets the Local Political Pot Boiling." September 1, 1873.

————. "Mrs. Mike M'Donald [*sic*] Illegally Resisting a Police Invasion." November 24, 1873.

————. "Mrs. O'Leary's Cow Cleared by City Council Meeting." October 6, 1997.

————. "No Money Can Be Borrowed from the Relief and Aid Society— The Mayor Wishes to Sell the Lake Park." December 25, 1873.

————. "An Outrage Upon a Colored Man." July 15, 1862.

————. "The Political Confederation." September 7, 1873.

————. "Report. First. Number of Establishments." January 30, 1854.

————. "Republicans Wake Up!" October 31, 1857.

————. "Riot in the Third Ward. Enrolling Officers Stoned and Injured." June 26, 1863.

————. "Rising from the Ooze." December 31, 1855.

————. "Ruffianism Rampant." September 28, 1874.

————. "The Scenes of October 9, 1871, Repeated on a Small Scale." July 15, 1874.

————. "The Sheriff and the Dieting of Prisoners." December 15, 1876.

————. "Statements and Affidavits to the Starting Point of the Great Fire." October 20, 1871.

————. "Tell of Threats by Mrs. M'Donald [*sic*]." March 2, 1907.

————. "Tells the Woes of Mrs. M'Donald [*sic*]." February 1, 1908.

————. "Was There Bribery." June 25, 1890.

————. "Which of the Aldermen Sold Their Votes for Dollars." July 8, 1886.

————. "Wife No. 1. Widow, No. 2 Repudiated." August 13, 1907.

————. "Will Recalls Murder Trial of Dora M'Donald [*sic*]." October 14, 1931.

————. "A Word with Irishmen." July 2, 1863.

Cincinnati Enquirer. "Her Face Was Covered in Blood." February 22, 1907.

————. "Two Thousand Howling 'Property-Owners' Visit the Board of Aldermen." January 18, 1872.

Daily Ohio Statesman. "Arlington's Minstrels." April 16, 1868.

Davenport Weekly Republican. "Mike M'Donald's [*sic*] Wife." October 12, 1889.

Galveston Daily News. "Mrs. M'Donald [*sic*] Reported to Have eloped with a Priest. Tells Why She Left Her Husband." October 10, 1889.

Inter-Ocean. "Carter Harrison. A Reception Tendered to Him Upon His Return to Chicago Last Night." March 7, 1879.

————. "County Gossip." June 5, 1877.

————. "Dora M'Donald [*sic*] to Be Placed on Trial Tomorrow." January 19, 1908.

————. "The Elections." November 4, 1873.

————. "Facts Which Show the Mayor's Meanness and Chief O'Donnell's Incompetency." January 7, 1880.

————. "Father Moysant." August 22, 1889.

————. "Here We Are Again. Mr. M.C. McDonald Re-enters Politics and Would Like to Be Mayor." January 4, 1893.

————. "Jealousy, Not Blackmail, Is State Charge." February 8, 1908.

————. "'Mike' McDonald's Wife Kills Artist in His Studio." February 22, 1907.

————. "Mrs. McDonald in Care of Doctors Is Regaining Senses." February 23, 1907.

————. "The North Side Cable Road." June 11, 1886.

————. "Preservation of Stone and Brick." January 1, 1887.

————. "The Saloon-Keepers' Ticket Victorious by Some 8,000 Majority." November 5, 1873.

————. "The Street Car Transfer." March 27, 1886.

New York Times. "Acquitted of a Charge of Attempted Murder." December 27, 1874.

———. "Eloped with a Priest." August 21, 1889.

Niagara This Week. "Irish Who Fled Potato Famine Landed in Niagara." March 20, 2009.

Omaha Daily Bee. "Mrs. M'Donald [*sic*] Returns. Mike Will Probably Forgive Her and Stop Divorce Proceedings." October 10, 1889.

Ottawa Journal. "The Face of Violence." October 21, 1961.

Pensacola News Journal. "Interesting Career of the Chicago Gambler Who Died Sunday." August 14, 1907.

Quad City Times. "A New Departure." May 17, 1873.

Rock Island Argus. "No Longer a Wife. Sequel to the Elopement of a Chicago Woman. Full Proof of Her Infidelity." November 23, 1889.

Salt Lake Herald Republican. "Shoots Artist. Rich Woman Held." February 22, 1907.

San Francisco Chronicle. "His Erring Wife. McDonald Explains Her Infatuation." August 22, 1889.

San Francisco Examiner. "Guerin's Slayer Raves in Prison." February 23, 1907.

Scholarly Commons. "Chicago's Great Boodle Trial." February 23, 2013.

Sioux City Journal. "You May Never Look Upon His Like Again." March 30, 1879.

Sterling Daily Gazette. "Twice Dishonored." August 21, 1889.

Wilkes-Barre Times. "Guerin's Slayer May Have Had Accomplice." February 26, 1907.

INDEX

ABOUT THE AUTHOR

Author of *Camp Douglas: Chicago's Civil War Prison*, Kelly Pucci also contributes to a variety of magazines, websites and newspapers. As a native Chicagoan, she enjoys exploring local history and has written about the city's ethnic restaurants, neighborhoods and museums.

Visit us at
www.historypress.com
....